W9-DES-033

Mysteries of Animal Intelligence

Sherry Hansen Steiger and Brad Steiger

TOR®

A TOM DOHERTY ASSOCIATES BOOK
NEW YORK

NOTE: If you purchased this book without a cover you should be aware that this book is stolen property. It was reported as "unsold and destroyed" to the publisher, and neither the author nor the publisher has received any payment for this "stripped book."

This is a work of fiction. All the characters and events portrayed in this book are either products of the author's imagination or are used fictitiously.

MYSTERIES OF ANIMAL INTELLIGENCE

Copyright © 1995 by Sherry Hansen Steiger and Brad Steiger

All rights reserved, including the right to reproduce this book, or portions thereof, in any form.

A Tor Book
Published by Tom Doherty Associates, LLC
175 Fifth Avenue
New York, NY 10010

www.tor.com

Tor® is a registered trademark of Tom Doherty Associates, LLC.

ISBN-13: 978-0-765-35748-9
ISBN-10: 0-765-35748-8

First mass market edition: August 1995
Second mass market edition: February 2007

Printed in the United States of America

0 9 8 7 6 5 4 3 2 1

"The basic concept on which goodness rests is reverence of life—the great mystery in which we find ourselves with all living things."

These are the words of the good Dr. Albert Schweitzer, the famous medical doctor who built and maintained his own hospital community in French Equitarial Africa. Dr. Schweitzer dedicated his entire life not only as a doctor, but as a teacher, builder, and friend to thousands of people who came to him for help.

Dr. Schweitzer believed the deeper we look into nature the more we recognize that it is full of life and profoundly a secret, yet we discover that we are united to all this life. "Let a person begin to think about the mystery of his life and the links which connect him with all of the life that fills the world, and he cannot but bring to bear upon his own life and all other life that comes within reach—the principle of reverence for life."

We cannot explain life. All we know is that life is a mystery, and we ought to be filled with awe and reverence for this mystery. It is in that same spirit that we the authors dedicate this book:—*To your heightened awareness and reverence for life.*

• Contents •

• Chapter One •

Our Mentor Mosie

As children, many of us secretly believed—or at least hoped—that certain animals, especially dogs and cats, could speak to us if they really wanted to communicate on a verbal level. That is why we are so pleased that our pet black Labrador, Moses, is a talking dog!

We are not going to claim that Moses speaks in discernible words that you, a stranger, might recognize as actual speech; but he does make distinctive grunting and moaning sounds whenever he wants fresh water, food, to go outside, or to express any number of other subjects important to him. He rarely barks when a friend or family member is at the door, or when the mail person delivers our mail—he simply comes to us and "tells" us that we have a visitor.

Sherry and Moses found each other at a yard sale in Phoenix, Arizona. While browsing among the assorted treasures in the yard and driveway, this cute, furry, pudgy, little black ball of a Labrador puppy kept following her, wrapping himself around her feet, and making bizarre grunting and moaning sounds.

The puppy's owner and Sherry both decided that it was Sherry's destiny to claim the dog. Sherry and her daughter Melissa christened him Moses after the Danny Glover character in the motion picture *Places in the Heart*. You may remember that whenever Sally Field, playing a widowed cotton farmer, gave Moses, the field hand (Glover), particular instructions with which he was not in harmony, he would walk away grunting, mumbling, and grumbling under his breath.

Although Moses had been trained as an outside dog for more than four years, we began bringing him inside with us when we moved in June 1991 to a wilder, still untamed part of the desert in Cave Creek, Arizona. The barren land was home to wily coyotes that would send a female in heat into the human habitations to lure male dogs out of their yards—whereupon hungry members of the coyote pack were waiting to pounce on the males who came to "court" the female . . . for dinner!

There were also herds of javelina (wild boars) nosing for something right under our bedroom windows, rattlesnakes here and there in our yard, to say nothing of the scorpions we picked out of the dishwasher or sink and the tarantulas on our doorstep! Needless to say, it was *their* territory, so we stayed there less than a year before we decided to let the desert critters have it all to themselves. But in the meantime, we certainly didn't want to offer up our pet Lab as their supper, so we decided we'd best bring Mosie Boy in. (We often call our black lab Mosie . . . perhaps so the neighbors don't think we have totally flipped our lids and are calling for Moses, the prophet of old.)

We were somewhat reluctant at first to bring the big moose of a dog in among delicate and breakable antiques and collectibles, especially since he was used to the great outdoors, but we followed our intuition, which told us that his seemingly exceptional intellect would allow him to adjust to proper behavior with little or no effort. We are happy to report that he not only did not disappoint us, he provided us with a firsthand education about the intelligence of dogs and the inexplicable joy of bonding and shared experiences with a very special kind of friend.

Brad had not paid Mosie a great deal of attention until this time. As an inveterate pet lover, Brad was still hurting over the loss of a very special dog and a most unique cat. They had been taken from him by unfortunate circumstances long ago, and he was hesitant to open up emotionally once again and risk the disappointment and loss that attend the death of a dear pet.

Suffice it to say, it did not take long for Moses and Brad to bond in deep and meaningful ways that soon had him referring to the big black Labrador as his "main man," so much so that around town people often refer to Brad as "that guy who always has his dog with him wherever he goes."

Almost at once Brad was struck by Mosie's remarkable intelligence. Sherry had once illustrated to him in their backyard in Scottsdale that she had only to direct him verbally—in a normal voice, with no gestures—to a tree, to a bush, or to other areas of the yard. She made it a point not to look or shift her eyes in the direction where she wanted Mosie to fetch an object, yet it seemed Mosie knew. It was as though Moses either understood the words or was mind reading—in any case, displaying more capabilities than we had given him credit for having.

Brad recalled the experiences of J. Allen Boone, the movie producer and former head of RKO studios, who had written movingly of his remarkable interaction with Strongheart, the internationally acclaimed champion German shepherd and movie personality. When Boone first gained possession of the dog, he was advised to treat him as if he were an intelligent human being. He was admonished to say nothing to him that he did not feel in his heart. And, interestingly, he was told to read something worthwhile to Strongheart each day.

Believing this to be sound advice, we decided to let Moses be included in our daily Bible study. We read the texts aloud, discussed them, and ended with prayer. In addition, we addressed Moses as we might one of our children, rather than a "pet." We certainly would never go so far as to set a place for him at the table, but in other subtle ways we treat him like one of the family.

An example would be something like this: "Well, Mosie, what do you say we go for a walk now?" Or "I think we're just about out of milk and bread, let's go to the store." Some might say we sound like doddering old fools talking to a dog; others, like our Scandinavian families, might say it's just our heritage of talking to ourselves and the dog just happens to be thrown in because he's there. But as for us, we have observed many exciting occurrences when we are convinced that Mosie has an expanded vocabulary. Often we are positive he understands almost everything we say.

One day as Brad sat working at the word processor, trying desperately to make the words come out in a sequence that would declare his intelligence rather than his confusion, the sounds of Moses chewing a leather toy directly behind him began to get on his nerves. It is a strange aspect of creative work that once one is really "into" the project, the sound of a cannon in the next room cannot disturb him or her. But until that miracle of complete absorption is achieved, the sound of a fly rubbing its wings on the windowsill can distract one's attention.

Without raising his voice, without turning to look at Moses, without even lifting his eyes from the keyboard of his word processor, Brad said in a firm but barely accented voice: "Moses, that is an exceedingly disgusting sound. I wish you would leave the room and go get a toy that doesn't make any sound at all."

The words were scarcely out of Brad's mouth when Moses got up, left the room for thirty seconds, and returned with a soft, quiet toy to occupy his boredom until Brad finished his work and could pay him some quality attention. Moses had done exactly as Brad had requested.

Brad was astonished, and when he reported the incident to Sherry, he emphasized the points that he had barely articulated the words and that he had not made any gestures to express his distaste for the slurpy dog sounds that Moses was making. He had not even turned to face the Labrador.

All things considered, it would seem that Moses would have had to have understood precisely what Brad had said—or *thought*—in order to comply with his wishes.

Since this incident, which occurred in August 1991, we have taken careful notice of a number of events in which Moses seemed to be able to perceive the full content and meaning of our conversations with him.

We realize, of course, that there would be no way on earth to convince an unrelenting skeptic that the above-mentioned incident was not just a startling coincidence. Moses had simply tired of the noisy toy at the exact moment that Brad had become annoyed by the sound of it and had exchanged the toys only to please his own personal doggy whim.

But we would ask those who regard dogs as more than highly animated gobs of hairy protoplasm to consider also the following experiment in canine teaching and its resultant display of canine reasoning.

Moses had grown into the habit of taking one of his toys with him between his jaws whenever he was let outside, and he would very often lose or misplace the toy while he was occupied with whatever task had brought him outdoors in the first place.

Brad quickly taught Moses to drop his toy at the doorway and to go outside with his jaws empty. Very soon it was no longer necessary for Brad to monitor the lesson. Moses would automatically drop the toy at the door and retrieve it on returning to the house.

It soon became apparent that Moses associated dropping his toy with going for a walk, going bye-bye in the car, and going potty. Consequently, it was not long at all before Moses would bring a toy to Brad and drop it noisily whenever he wished to go outside for any of the above reasons. If Brad ignored the dropping of the first toy, Moses would fetch another, lift his jaws higher, and drop the toy louder than before.

What began as a lesson in not scattering toys soon became transformed into Moses' reasoning that the dropping of a toy communicated his desire to go outside for recreation or to obey a call of nature.

That seems clearly to be an act of intelligent reasoning on the part of a dog and the adaptation of a process that had been learned for one purpose to serve a different kind of function—in this case, communication.

Then there is the question of emotions. If animals have intellect, do they also have feelings? Sherry's mom, Lorraine Lippold, tells how their German shepherd, Guard, used to somehow sneak in at night while she was sound asleep and gently manage to get under her pillow—without disturbing her in the slightest. What was under the pillow? Mom Lippold always had a cough drop or two tucked under her pillow so they'd be close at hand if she needed them during the night. Guard evidently found these pretty tasty, so periodically she would ever so quietly snitch one.

Mom would make the bed and notice the missing

goodies and scold Guard. Now, that's not so difficult to imagine: a dog that liked what seemed to be candy. But to us, the neatest part of the story was that after the first time Guard was scolded, she began replacing what she took with something. She would always leave one of her toys in place of the lozenges!

Is it too far-fetched to think that Guard felt so bad about taking something for nothing that she left an offering to "pay" for her treat?

At other times, whenever Mom and Dad Lippold were packing to go on a trip, Mom would leave the room to get something from another room. She'd come back to pack it and Guard would have put all her toys in the suitcase. No matter how many times Mom would take them out, Guard would always manage to catch Mom off guard and sneak them all back in, hiding them under the clothes. Was Guard making sure Mom got the message not to forget to take her wonderful dog too? Guard was very persistent, as good as saying, Can I come too, please, please?

Throughout this book we have many amazing stories—all of them true. We interject the latest ongoing research about the intelligence of animals. We also examine many issues surrounding intelligence, such as: do animals have emotions, do they feel sadness and joy, can animals think and reason?

We'll let you be the judge. We urge you to examine the actions and idiosyncrasies of your own pets and perhaps *all* animals with a new perspective.

Carefully observe how many ways those pets or animals might be attempting to communicate with humans. We think you may experience joy and happiness, if not from believing they have intelligence, simply from the beauty and order of the web of life of which we all are a part.

• Chapter Two •

Not-So-Dumb Animals

Tradition has it that a Great Dane named Ritz Kent Arthur William John de Ritz faithfully attended classes at Hillsdale College in Michigan each day for four years and graduated as a member of the class of 1940. The academic pooch wore a mortarboard as it pranced across the stage on graduation day to receive his degrees of Doctor of Dogmatics and Master of Caninical Law.

While we sense a bit of collegiate humor here, we also cannot help pondering what motivated de Ritz the Great Dane to show up for classes each day—and we certainly wonder how much the cultured canine absorbed from each pedagogical lecture.

Recent research on animal intelligence indicates that old de Ritz, Hillsdale class of 1940—and the entire gamut of the animal species—may know a whole lot more than we've ever thought possible. In the last decade or so, laboratory tests designed to evaluate animal intelligence have once again raised the age-old query: how intelligent are the animals over which our traditions of science and religion give us dominion? New studies yield the somewhat uncomfortable conclusions that various members of the animal kingdom are far from "dumb" animals.

Warren Thomas, coauthor of *Dolphin Conferences, Elephant Midwives, and Other Astonishing Facts About Animals*, states that even the elephant, too often casually dismissed as a great, ungainly creature of little wit, is revealed as possessing many behavior traits amazingly similar to those of humans. They enter a rather elaborate courtship with a prospective mate; walk trunk-in-trunk, as if holding hands; mate in private; and use older herd females as midwives to deliver their babies.

Dolphins, according to Thomas, appear to conduct formal conferences, coming together in a tight circle with their heads facing one another, before they make any decision that will affect the other members of their group. They even take turns talking the problem out before the final agreement has been reached.

Only a few short years ago, the lowly opossum was considered a "primitive, living fossil," with, as Jamestown's Captain John Smith wrote in 1612, "a head like a swine and a tail like a rat." Biologists scorned the creature as being a rudimentary beastie, more reptilian than typically mammalian.

But in the April/May 1993 issue of *National Wildlife*, Doug Stewart quotes Harvard biologist Donna Holmes defending the opossum as being capable of complex social interactions, marking home ranges, establishing pecking orders, and, on occasions, even sharing nests.

Controlled laboratory experiments seeking to determine animal intelligence use mazes or puzzle boxes, or have their subjects push or peck the right symbol to obtain a food reward.

These methods and similar ones are unsatisfactory, and at best may rate only the intelligence level and response time of the individual subject. For not only do the levels between species vary but there can be great differences between individuals within each species. This explains why zoologists cannot agree on a specific, uniform test to measure animal intelligence.

Studies at Columbia University's Animal Laboratory list the animals behind humans as follows:

1. The great apes (with the chimpanzee at the top), monkeys
2. The carnivores, which include the dog, cat, fox, raccoon, lion, tiger, and bear
3. The grazing animals, among which are the elephant, horse, pig, cow, deer, and zebra
4. The birds, followed by reptiles, amphibians, and fishes

Research at the University of Georgia resulted in a different scale. They place the pig just below the fox and raccoon and ahead of the dog, followed by sheep, birds, rats, rabbits, cats, horses, and guinea pigs.

The Georgia report goes on to state that humans are probably more to blame for the poor intelligence showings of the dog, cat, and horse than the animals themselves: "Domesticated life has dulled their natural curiosity prowess," commented a spokesperson for the study.

On and on it goes. The intelligence of various animals is rated differently in a wide variety of tests. And new research constantly requires scientists to revise their studies and their test results.

Early in the 1970s, Beatrice and R. Allen Gardner taught a young female chimpanzee to master 150 hand gestures in simplified American Sign Language.

About the same time, psychologist David Premack had great success in teaching a female chimpanzee named Sarah to communicate with metal-backed plastic chips that she could stick to a magnetic board.

Duane Rumbaugh, Georgia State University, and the Yerkes Regional Primate Research Center of Emory University taught a chimp named Lana to communicate by a system of geometric symbols on a computer keyboard.

And when it comes to motherly love, that most "human" of emotions, Dr. Mavis Newell, a lecturer at the Center for the Study of Human Behavior in Canberra, Australia, commented in spring 1991 that as a species we humans have a great deal to *learn* from various animals about maternal love and dedication to our young.

"While today human children are being harmed by self-indulgent women who are mothers in name only, you won't find a battered newborn or a crack baby in the den or the nest of a wild animal," said Dr. Newell, who went on to cite dolphin mothers as a perfect example of selfless motherly love. "[Dolphin mothers] have been known to attempt suicidal rescues of their young rather than abandon them to the nets of tuna fishermen."

Anyone who has seen dolphins perform at such places as Sea World cannot help wondering just how intelligent these graceful creatures really are. Controversial as the allegation might be in certain hallowed halls of learning, some scientists have speculated that dolphins may be even more intelligent than humans. At this point in our investigation of animal intelligence, we feel it may be safer to say that we have not begun to know the full capabilities of our sea-dwelling cousins.

There are an ever-increasing number of dolphin research centers worldwide that are revealing startling information about these mysterious mammals.

At the Gulf Stream Research Center on Florida's Grassy Key, Miami psychologist David Nathanson is doing groundbreaking research that documents tremendous improvement with disabled patients who have interacted with dolphins. Children with Downs syndrome, hydrocephalus, cerebral palsy, muscular dystrophy, and head or spinal-cord injuries have made significant progress after sessions with the healers from the sea.

Amanda Morris, a member of Britain's Royal Air Force, has found that Sharkey, Betty, and Lottie, three dolphins at an experimental animal park in Great Britain, have contributed greatly to her fight against a deadly brain tumor. Three years ago, Amanda was told that she would die within a month. Rather than giving in to despair, she turned to her dolphin friends.

"They nudge me and tow me about the pool," Amanda said, explaining the seagoing mammals' healing technique. "They talk to me by clicking and high-pitched whistling. I know that they are making me better. They're also giving me the will to live and hope for the future."

Peter Bloom, curator of the animal park that houses the dolphins, was frank in his admiration for the process of healing that he has been able to witness firsthand. While Bloom admits there may be no presently acceptable scientific explanation for what Amanda has accomplished with her dolphin healers, he pragmatically assesses the situation by stating that if one receives healing and happiness from doing something, "then it makes sense to do it."

In the March 1992 issue of *Reader's Digest*, an article by Per Ola and Emily D'Aulaire entitled "Playful Genius of the Sea" quotes Louis Herman, psychologist and director of the Marine Mammal Laboratory, Hawaii, who admits to having been completely astonished by new research with dolphins.

Herman recounted a particular experiment in which a dolphin surprised the researchers by spontaneously deriving "a totally untrained, invented response." He adds: "We never dreamed the animal would 'think' the problem through like that."

The ability to "think things through" is the criterion that scientists have used for centuries as a safe dividing line to separate humans from their fellow creatures on planet Earth. It was heretofore believed that no animal had the capacity for reasoning. Now a wealth of research with dolphins and a wide variety of other animals reveals a humanlike learning capability.

"They plan. They deceive. They solve problems in ways that demand more than basic instinct. The search has begun for the creatures' inner lives"—so reads a subhead in a November 1, 1993, issue of *Newsweek* magazine. The article reports research with all kinds of animals, from beavers and green-backed herons to otters and chimps, drawing the same conclusion about all of them—that they think.

In the past, scientists who dared suggest such theories of animals were shunned, but now scientists are beginning to change their thinking about animal thinking. The evidence is so overwhelming that animals do indeed plot and plan and solve problems that it has created a whole new profound issue to tackle—do animals think about thinking?

Some researchers such as Dale Peterson and Jane Goodall have written numerous books on their findings. In *Visions of Caliban*, Peterson and Goodall stress what they say is an inescapable conclusion from their research that chimpanzees are "moral beings" imbued with many of the same personal and psychological characteristics as humans.

In Stanley Coren's *The Intelligence of Dogs, Canine Consciousness and Capabilities*, the author states that dogs have a much richer and more sophisticated language than we have ever imagined. A psychologist and dog trainer himself, Coren states rather matter-of-factly that we would understand animals quite a bit better if we accepted the fact that they have simple felings, fears, desires, and beliefs, and make plans, have goals, and the like. He states, "How can anyone live with a dog without thinking, 'the dog is thirsty and wants some water when it stands over an empty water dish, barks, and then pushes it toward you with its nose?' How can one avoid thinking, 'the dog wants to go out,' when it barks at you and paws at the front door?" He goes on to cite many other perfect examples.

Bonita Bergin, director of Canine Companions for Independence, teaches eighty-nine different commands to the dogs she trains to assist disabled people. Dogs trained by Ms. Bergin have mastered hitting elevator buttons, turning light switches on and off, retrieving objects that have been dropped, and getting food out of the refrigerator.

What truly impresses this accomplished dog trainer, however, is not so much the lengthy string of commands that they are taught to obey as the sense of responsibility that the animals develop. For example, when something, let us say a book, is dropped on the floor, a working dog doesn't automatically pick it up. It looks up to see if the person *wants* the object retrieved. That, in her opinion, is intelligence.

Vicki Hearne, an English professor and trainer of dogs and horses in a kennel in rural Connecticut, is quoted as saying, "What's interesting is what happens to your relationship with an animal as the training progresses. 'Sit,' 'Come,' 'Stay,' 'Stand,' 'Heel,' and 'Down' don't mean the formal movements. . . . What they mean is, 'You and I stand now in a certain relation-ship to the rest of the world. We consult each other about things that come up.' " (*Newsweek*, May 23, 1988)

All of these considerations and the many more we explore in the rest of this book lead us to question not only the learning capabilities or intelligence of animals but whether, as Jane Goodall stated of the chimps, some animals may be moral beings as well. If we were to view animals as thinking, sentient beings it would not just be the ethnologists busy re-examining the place of animals in our world. We would all need to consider more seriously our interaction with them.

• Chapter Three •

The Remarkable Affinity between Animals and Their Owners

Harvard professor E. O. Wilson, the father of sociobiology and author of *The Diversity of Life* (Harvard University Press), maintains that human beings inherit a tendency to feel an affinity and awe for all living things, which explains why so many of us fill our homes with plants and pets. However, he warns, when we wantonly destroy aspects of the natural world around us, we "court spiritual disaster."

Wilson reminds us that the human brain evolved into its present form over a period of about two million years. Throughout all that time, we existed in an intimate relationship with the natural environment. Today we are still instinctively drawn toward the wilderness and to an interaction with animals.

In an article in the November 30, 1992, issue of *U.S. News & World Report*, Bob Holmes detailed supportive research for Wilson's theory of a genetic spirituality, an affinity for the natural world that he terms *biophilia*.

In one experiment, people from settings as varied as the urban United States and rural Bali were asked to rate the appeal of a number of photographs depicting a wide variety of landscapes. Overwhelmingly, the favorite choices were of open, grassy environments with water and scattered trees "just like the savanna habitat that was home for milleniums to ancient human ancestors."

University of Washington zoologist Gordon Orians and psychologist Judith Heerwagen found that landscape painters typically alter their finished scenes of the actual terrain by adding water and open forest, thereby making their pictures more savannalike. Orians and Heerwagen also discovered that most people prefer low-branching trees that are wider than they are tall, a shape characteristic of trees on the African plains.

Roger Ulrich, an environmental psychologist at Texas A & M University's College of Architecture, found rural and urban dwellers alike preferred almost any scene of nature to almost any scene of a city environment that lacked vegetation or water. Ulrich also discovered that his subjects displayed brain-wave patterns characteristic of "relaxed alertness," or the alpha state, when they were shown photographs of vegetation and water. (Extensive research has revealed that when the alpha brain-wave state is reached, there seems to be a conducive mental state for heightened learning and creativity.)

In the article "Living with Nature" (Betsy Carpenter with Bob Holmes, *U.S. News & World Report*, November 30, 1992), E. O. Wilson is quoted as insisting that until we humans better comprehend "the depth and the complexity of nature's hold on the human spirit, continuing to raze habitat is extraordinarily risky." In other words, as long as we continue to level or destroy various environments that are the natural homes or habitats of many creatures (such as the rainforest in Brazil), we could be asking for trouble.

While today it may only be mostly field biologists such as Wilson who are suffering nightmares about the destruction of eco-systems and the extinction of beloved plant and animal species, in time, he warns, many other thoughtful humans may find themselves troubled and grief-stricken. The loss of biodiversity on the planet, Wilson says, may be "the folly our descendents are least likely to forgive us."

It may be such an ancient affinity for the animals in our environment that can account in at least some small way for such remarkable stories of human and animal interaction as the following:

H. Rider Haggard's Dream of His Dying Dog

H. Rider Haggard may have been best known for novels of fantastic adventure, such as *She* and *King Solomon's Mines*, but he was also recognized by those who knew him well as a man with a great fondness for animals.

One night, according to his own account of the incident, the author was experiencing a terrible nightmare; and he was greatly relieved when his wife awakened him, thus redeeming his consciousness from the grip of the dreadful nocturnal drama.

As he was awakening, the shadowy residue of the nightmare completely disappeared from his brain—but he experienced the strange phenomenon of perceiving yet another dream in those few seconds before he returned to full wakefulness.

He dreamed that Bob, a favorite black retriever dog that he had always prized for its good nature and intelligence, was lying terribly injured in some brush near water. In Haggard's dream, the dog was attempting to speak to him in words. Then, failing at verbal communication, the retriever transmitted the knowledge directly to the author's brain that it was dying.

Once again Haggard's wife brought him to full waking consciousness by asking him why he was making such weird noises. The author replied without hesitation that he had just had another dream that old Bob was dying and was trying to tell him about his plight.

Soon after his unpleasant evening of nightmares, someone brought Haggard old Bob's collar. It had been found on a railway bridge.

Three days later, the retriever's body was sighted in the river beneath the bridge. The author was saddened to learn that his vision had been accurate. Old Bob had evidently been struck by a train and thrown into the brush near the riverbank.

Prince Crossed the English Channel to Find His Master in the Trenches at Armentières

Kevin Okeefe joined the British army during the onset of World War I. In order that his wife, Colleen, and his dog, Prince, would not be left alone in Ireland for the duration, he saw them safely situated with relatives in Hammersmith, London, before he entered the ranks of the doughboys.

Kevin was with the earliest British contingents to be sent to France, and his unit was soon in the thickest of the fighting. After a time, he was allowed weekend leave from the fury of trench warfare to visit his wife in London. Although he knew that he could enjoy only the very briefest respite from the mud, the blood, and the barbed wire, Kevin made every moment count with the two beings he loved most.

After Kevin had returned to the trenches in France, Prince was inconsolable. He refused all food and barely drank any water. Then came the terrible morning when Colleen discovered that Prince had disappeared.

"I've searched everywhere I know to look," she told a member of Kevin's family. "Prince has run off. I don't know how I can break the news to Kevin. He'll be terribly upset, and I don't want to demoralize the poor lad as he suffers in those wretched trenches."

Colleen decided to wait ten days before she made the formal declaration of Prince's disappearance. And in those desperate days, she renewed her efforts to discover the dog's whereabouts. At last, realizing full well that it was the honest thing to do, she wrote to her husband the sad news that Prince had run off a few days after he had returned to the front.

Imagine Colleen's astonishment when she finally received a reply from Kevin that Prince was with him in the trenches at Armentières.

Somehow, in a way impossible for conventional knowledge to elucidate, Prince deciphered the unfamiliar maze of London's streets and negotiated 70 miles of unknown countryside, as well as a significant body of water—the English Channel. The shortest distance across the Channel is about 20 miles, and at its widest is 100 miles.

According to the records, Prince arrived at the trenches at Armentières at a time when the British line was under a barrage of heavy shellfire. Ducking bursting shells, dodging erupting earth, and evading deadly tear gas, Prince was able to catch his master's personal scent among an army of half a million Englishmen.

"Never was a dog so well-named and titled as this one," declared a trenchmate of Okeefe's when he beheld Prince at his master's side.

How Is It Possible for a Dog to Find Someone So Far Away?

Although scientists do not yet fully understand *how*, dogs have a remarkable ability of heightened scent. This has been common knowledge for centuries, making many dogs valuable rescuers, crime fighters, and finders of people, places, and things. It is common for the police and others to rely on dogs to track criminals, find missing persons, detect smuggled or hidden illegal substances, and so on.

As incredible as it may seem, one of the breeds best known for "sniffing" ability is the droopy-eyed, floppy-eared bloodhound, which has a nose up to three million times more sensitive than a human's. Bloodhounds have tracked down criminals and located missing persons over distances of many hundreds of miles. This uncanny ability seems almost supernatural, as one observes the rapidity with which they accomplish their assigned task.

Not only the bloodhound but Newfoundlands, St. Bernards, German shepherds, and Labrador retrievers are among the breeds that seem gifted with this keen, finely tuned sense of smell. All they seem to need is to get a whiff of something personal, such as an object belonging to the person being tracked, and they immediately embark on the path of this invisible smell.

One possible explanation for this tracking ability has to do with human cells. As strange as it sounds, a human being sheds some fifty million skin cells each day, and they are scattered behind us wherever we go. One theory is that a dog, such as a bloodhound, can smell the microscopic organisms that feed on these skin flakes, if not the flakes themselves, with their supersensitive snouts!

Pet Cat Awakens Family and Saves Them from Lethal Fumes

One evening in April 1973, Michael Lousada and his two children were asleep in their home in Woburn Sands when fumes that would most certainly have proved to be lethal began to leak from a gas-fueled heating boiler. Somehow, to their everlasting gratitude, the Lousadas' cat became alerted to the silent, deadly danger moving inexorably through the home.

The cat began to mew and scratch noisily and persistently until each family member had been awakened and made aware of the fumes.

"Weakened by the gas and very near to coma, Mr. Lousada was just able to help his children out of the house," author Dennis Bardens said in writing about the case. "The three fully recovered after a stay in the local hospital."

The Dog Who Could Read Egyptian Train Schedules

In his book *Dogs: Man's Best Friend*, Captain Trapman tells us of Peter, a most talented dog who had somehow acquired a knowledge of how to change trains—even in the formidable confusion of the Cairo depot.

As the story goes, Peter, a bull terrier, was the pride of a Mr. Jobson, a British government official stationed in Upper Egypt circa 1901. Jobson delighted in bringing his dog with him wherever he traveled, and he frequently brought Peter along on the fifteen-hour journey to Cairo. Other of Jobson's companions noted that the bull terrier would settle himself comfortably in a train seat and never once look out the window.

A career move eventually transferred Jobson to

Demanhour, about three hours' journey from Cairo. On one occasion, a situation arose in which it was necessary for him to leave for Cairo, but it was not convenient for him to bring along his constant canine companion. A very grumpy and out-of-sorts Peter was left behind.

As it turned out, Peter would have none of staying alone at home. Somehow he managed to board a train to Cairo, and when he reached that familiar destination, he changed platforms, switched trains, and set out on the fifteen-hour trip to their old home in Upper Egypt. Peter's bull terrier logic had convinced him that the master must have returned to the site of his previous tour of duty.

Although Peter had never bothered to look out of a window during his many previous trips back and forth between Upper Egypt and Cairo, it seemed as if he uncannily knew when to leave the train and to search out Jobson's old haunts at his previously assigned station. It was obvious that Peter's master was not there, so without wasting any more time, he headed immediately for the train depot.

It would be quite understandable if the exhausted dog did not bother to look out the window during the fifteen-hour trip back to Cairo. We may assume that he got some much-needed rest so that he would be fresh for tracking his master on the teeming streets of Cairo.

Several of Jobson's friends and acquaintances were astonished to see Peter poke his head in their doors. "What on earth are you doing here, old man?" he was asked again and again. "Where is Jobson, your master?"

The bull terrier displayed visible disappointment when he found Jobson at none of his usual ports of call. Where on earth was that wandering master of his?

The remarkably resourceful terrier made his way back to the Cairo train depot, waited patiently for three hours before the proper engine arrived, then entrained once again for Demanhour.

Here, at last, Peter was rewarded for his persistence. Jobson had returned home and had been worried sick about the mysterious disappearance of his faithful dog.

Although this story may sound like an inspired piece of fiction, we are told that all the details were confirmed at the time by careful inquiries conducted by Jobson and his friends.

Devoted Dog Stands Vigil over Dead Master's Body for Three Months

When the collie was found, he was so weak from hunger that he couldn't even stand. But the loyal dog had completed his vigil. He had stood guard over his dead master's body for nearly three months.

Police constable Martin Coups told journalists that searchers had found Ruswarp, the fourteen-year-old collie mix, lying barely conscious beside the body of Graham Nuttall, forty-one, who had apparently suffered a heart attack while hiking in the frost-covered hills of central Wales in January 1990. Although the dog may have left the body of his master long enough to hunt down small game, it was believed that Ruswarp had lived primarily off his own body fat and water from the spring where his master had died.

Nuttall, a bachelor and a devoted railroad enthusiast, had named his faithful canine companion after a train depot in North Yorkshire.

Police Constable Coups said that his heart had gone out to the dog who was too feeble to stand, let alone walk, so he carried him 5 miles to an inn. Fearful that Ruswarp would die in his arms, the officer gave him some chocolate candy—which he wolfed right down.

Ruswarp was taken to a veterinary clinic in Llandrindod Wells, where accomplished veterinarians treated him for anemia and malnutrition.

Although he had been in a pitiful, confused condition when he was brought to the clinic, Ruswarp soon rallied and became something of a regional hero. Everyone was quick to note that loyal friends such as Ruswarp are hard to find.

• Chapter Four •

The Incredible Wilderness Challenge of Irwin and Orient

Here is the wilderness challenge. Let's see how you would respond.

You are challenged to hike the entire length of the Appalachian Trail—a total of 2,144 tough miles through thick forests, waterfalls, rivers, and mountain ranges. And everything that you will need for daily necessities on the grueling trek must be stuffed into a 90-pound pack on your back.

You'll pass? You say that the challenge sounds to you like something only an experienced camper and woodsman would undertake? And then he would probably want at least two or three equally proficient outdoorsmen on his team, right?

When fifty-one-year-old Bill Irwin accepted the wilderness challenge, he had never hiked or camped before in his life, and his only companion was his Seeing Eye dog, Orient.

Yes, that's correct. Bill Irwin is blind.

In March 1990, in perhaps one of the most astounding self-imposed challenges ever undertaken by a handicapped person, Irwin strapped a 90-pound pack to his 210-pound frame and set out on the trail from Georgia to Maine. For the entire length of the arduous march, his only teammate would be his faithful German shepherd guide dog, thus proclaiming Irwin's confidence and trust in Orient's intelligence and resourcefulness.

The two adventurers began their trek in Dahlonega, Georgia, on a day when a driving rain sent a chill through both of them.

When they camped that first night, Irwin had no way of determining if they were lost or on the correct path.

With only Orient to guide him and no other human to read a map or to confirm directions, Irwin knew that he had no choice other than to continue walking with firm determination.

That first night Orient curled up next to him, barking or growling whenever he heard the strange night sounds of wild animals in the forest. The big German shepherd would continue to lie protectively next to his owner on every subsequent night of the wilderness journey.

On the third day of their trek, they chanced upon some hikers who, much to Irwin's joy and peace of mind, assured them that they were, indeed, following the Appalachian Trail.

To some degree, Irwin had been able to prepare himself for the ordeal by listening to cassette tapes that described the wonders of the famous trail. Friends who had some familiarity with the hike also did their best to paint substantial word pictures of the various terrains Irwin and Orient would encounter.

They had not been on the trail too long before the German shepherd developed painful, running sores on his back from carrying a supplementary pack.

Irwin knew that the sturdy dog needed time to heal, so he added Orient's pack to his own.

For three weeks, he recalled, he lugged Orient's pack, struggling along, stumbling, being tripped by roots and knocked down by low tree branches.

Irwin admitted that he had felt genuine fear when a late-season hurricane came roaring inland from the Atlantic ocean.

He remembered the wind howling, tearing branches from the trees, and ripping the trees themselves from the ground. While the lightning and thunder seemed to shake the very ground around them, the adventurer and his loyal canine companion huddled under Irwin's poncho.

Weeks turned into months as the stalwart duo maintained a steady pace along the trail. Occasionally, they would meet other hikers, who would confirm or deny the correctness of their course.

Before they left for their trip, Irwin had arranged for his friends to mail food he had packaged into boxes to specific post offices in towns he would pass through. He had meticulously packed each box with supplies that would last for at least five days at a time. Irwin had planned to leave the forest every five days to venture out to the predesignated post office to pick up the next box of food and supplies. This well-thought-out plan would make the going much lighter for such an extensive trip—there wouldn't be so much weight to carry around because the five-day packs would be much more manageable.

About halfway on the 2,144-mile hike, a misstep on a slippery rock in a riverbed sent Irwin sprawling. The awful snapping sounds and the sharp pains in his torso provided him with the unwelcome news that he had broken several ribs.

For the next two weeks, Irwin said, each step, each breath brought him severe pain.

To make matters worse, he had already lost all of his nails from his toes rubbing against his boots while edging his way down long, steep stretches on the trail.

There were some days, Irwin concedes, when he assessed his broken ribs, his painful feet, the discomfort of cold, wet weather, and began to laugh at himself. But, he insists, he refused to quit.

He had known at the outset that he would face pain, hardships, and many days of inclement weather.

He also knew that he would never give up.

Perhaps one of his most harrowing experiences occurred in November, when he and Orient had nearly achieved their goal of conquering the Appalachian Trail. Irwin lost his footing in a stream swollen by heavy rains, and he was dragged by the swift-moving current toward what he would later learn was a 40-foot waterfall.

Somehow he managed to grab hold of a rock, and then, moving from rock to rock, he pulled himself out of the stream.

When Irwin and Orient finally reached the pathway's end in November, it had taken them eight exhausting and painful months to attain their goal.

Their remarkable achievement marked the first time that a blind person had ever completed the trek, thus heralding yet another heroic effort accomplished through the mutually supportive partnership of a man and his dog.

• Chapter Five •

These Pets' Quick Thinking Saved Human Lives

Foxy Rang the Bell and Brought Help for His Mistress

On December 8, 1966, a small fox terrier was responsible for bringing aid to its injured mistress, Mrs. W. Z. Robinette, eighty-four, of Gate City, Virginia.

Mrs. Robinette had fallen on the concrete walkway in front of her home and had broken her hip. Unable to move, the elderly woman lay helpless in her pain. Her feeble cries for help failed to elicit any type of response from her nearby neighbors.

Then Foxy, her terrier, bounded into view.

Cocking his head quizzically from side to side, Foxy seemed to be thinking the situation over very carefully.

"I . . . need . . . help," Mrs. Robinette managed to say in her pain.

Foxy whined his sympathy in apparent understanding, and began to pace nervously around the form of his fallen mistress. Suddenly his attention seemed to be directed to an outside dinner bell. Mrs. Robinette followed Foxy's intent gaze and groaned aloud—this time in despair and frustration rather than pain. Because Foxy had taken canine delight in occasionally grabbing the rope and ringing the bell, she had recently tied the rope up out of the terrier's reach so that he might not annoy the neighbors.

The new height of the rope seemed not to bother Foxy's planning. Although he had not rung the bell since his mistress had scolded him and tied the rope out of his reach, he ignored the taboo in light of the present emergency. Do you think it was possible that he could have understood or presupposed that all would be forgiven if he were to accomplish a supercanine leap and make the bell ring for all it was worth?

Summoning hidden resources of energy, Foxy leaped 3 feet into the air, snatched the rope in his teeth, and brought forth a resounding ringing of the bell. Again and again, the little fox terrier jumped high and yanked the rope with his teeth.

Foxy's whole body wagged along with his tail as if he knew he had done a good thing. The nearest neighbor came running to his mistress' side.

The concerned neighbor immediately summoned an ambulance, and Mrs. Robinette was on her way to a hospital for treatment. While she recovered under medical care, Foxy was cared for in a manner befitting a hero.

Lucy the Cat Would Not Back Down from the Rattlesnake

On a quiet October afternoon in 1990, Lucy the cat positioned herself between her owner's infant son,

Adam, and a 4-foot-long rattlesnake that had somehow managed to enter their home in Laguna Niguel, California.

Holly Lenz had been relaxing with a book in their backyard after she had put Adam down for a nap. Puzzled by the strange buzzing and hissing sound she heard coming from inside the house, she was terrified when she discovered the deadly serpent being held at bay by Lucy, who refused to back down and permit the snake access to Adam's bedroom.

A call to 911 brought police and an animal control officer as reinforcements for the brave cat.

Rufus Dragged His 300-Pound Owner to Safety

On a frosty morning in December 1992, fifty-year-old Andi Troast of Paupack, Pennsylvania, found out that the luckiest day of her life was the one when she took in a scrawny, dirty, stray dog that she named Rufus. For on that awful morning in December, Mrs. Troast fell on the ice, severed her foot, and would have bled to death if her sheepdog-Labrador buddy had not dragged her to safety.

Mrs. Troast had been scattering some feed for the deer that frequented the wooded area near her isolated rural home when she suddenly slipped on the ice. Her left foot had sailed out from under her when she fell backward, but her right foot had stayed firmly in place, anchored by a chunk of ice.

Once her senses had focused through the blinding pain, she was shocked to see that she had literally snapped her foot off. In horror that surpassed her agony, she perceived that it remained attached to her leg only by a thin strip of flesh and some ligaments.

Desperation endowed her with the strength to begin inching toward her house, moving backward over the frozen earth, leaving a crimson trail of blood on the snow.

After an eternity of torture, Mrs. Troast managed to reach her doorstep, growing weaker by the second from loss of blood. Somehow she had to call for help, but the greatest hurdle to surpass still lay before her. The door to her home was closed, and the latch was out of her reach.

Then, through the fog of pain and shock, she heard Rufus barking inside. Although she knew that it would be a miracle if her dog could understand the complications of the ghastly dilemma that she faced, Mrs. Troast also knew that the hope of a miracle was about all that she had left.

There are many stories in which dogs other than Lassie, Rin Tin Tin, and Benji of Hollywood fame have opened doors with ease. We've seen dogs do this and perhaps Mrs. Troast had too. At any rate, she commanded Rufus to stand on his hind legs. Rufus obeyed, then struck at the latch with his paws until he had managed to open the door.

Once outside, Rufus grabbed his mistress' collar and began to tug at her. Mrs. Troast put her arms around her determined dog, fearing that there was no way that he would be able to pull her 300 pounds over the doorstep and into the house.

Somehow, from some source of power and energy, Rufus found the strength to haul Mrs. Troast over the doorstep, drag her across the living room, and continue into the bedroom, where his mistress managed to call for help. Then Rufus cuddled against her and stayed there until the ambulance arrived.

Mrs. Troast said that she knew that Rufus had saved her life, and because of him, she stated, "I'm going to watch my grandchildren grow up."

Oscar Told His Owner That Her Baby Was Choking to Death

In the fall of 1990, Oscar the cat was faced with a dilemma. It was as though he knew that there was something wrong with his owner's baby, yet he also knew that he was not permitted near the infant's crib and he was not allowed to jump up on the furniture. So how was he going to alert his mistress, Kandy, that her Anthony was in danger?

Time was wasting. Oscar began a fierce yowling and boldly jumped up on the kitchen counter near the spot where Kandy was doing dishes.

All he got was a scolding and a quick brush-off. After repeating the maneuver with the same results and no meaningful communication accomplished, Oscar appeared to reason that he must take desperate measures—so he gave his mistress a nip on the leg.

Later, Kandy Phillips of Modesto, California, would admit that the bite had only been hard enough to let her know that Oscar was really serious about something.

Once he had her attention, Oscar ran to the bedroom where four-month-old Anthony was sleeping, violated another house rule by jumping up on the changing table, then, truly throwing caution to the winds, he bounded directly into the baby's crib.

At last he had accomplished his mission. When Kandy reached the crib, her eyes widened in awful comprehension of the impending tragedy that Oscar had been doing his darnedest to avert. Little Anthony was lying on his side, his face purple, his eyes tightly shut. He had spit up in his sleep, choked on the vomit—and he did not appear to be breathing.

Relying on mother's inspiration, Kandy at last managed to find the position that brought air back into her baby's lungs. And when the time of crisis had passed, she realized that if Oscar had not summoned her to Anthony's crib, her four-month-old son would most certainly have choked to death.

King Knew Where to Go to Save His Own Life

Some years ago, James Hamilton of Georgetown, Kentucky, had a dog named King, who seemed to take keen interest in his surroundings and in the process of life's ebb and flow in his immediate environment.

One day, when King was struck by an automobile and injured, the clever canine seemed to know exactly what to do. He dragged himself to a veterinary hospital.

Somehow Sarge Knew to Bite the Electrical Wire in Half

Ben Smith of Lynwood, Washington, recalled how the lives of his brother and his uncle had been saved by the quick action taken by their pet bulldog, Sarge.

The incident occurred back in the 1930s when electricity was still new in the farmlands of Oregon. Ben's five-year-old brother and his uncle were walking in the rain when they approached an electric fence that had been designed to corral cattle. The boy, being a typical inquisitive child, decided to touch the fence to see if it would really shock a person in the rain. Normally, the charge of an electric livestock fence would give off just enough of a shock to repel a cow and tingle the finger of a human. What the boy and his uncle did not realize, however, was that their neighbor had constructed his homemade electric fence by using a 220-volt direct current, which would pack a tremendous wallop.

When the unsuspecting boy put his hand on the wire, the shock was so great that he could not let go. When his uncle saw what had occurred and attempted to release him, they became "frozen" together by the high-voltage electricity.

The man and his nephew would both surely have died within minutes if it had not been for some remarkable awareness on the part of the bulldog.

"With those powerful bulldog jaws, he bit the wire in half," Ben Smith said. "It was as if Sarge knew that he had only a split second to do the deed or he, too, would be frozen by the electrical charge and become as helpless as they were."

Although the courageous Sarge managed to accomplish the heroic and selfless act, he could not possibly have moved fast enough to escape the effects of the powerful electrical charge. The bulldog fell dead the instant his jaws snapped the wire, and the man and boy survived only because of Sarge's self-sacrificing act.

The doctor who later examined the boy said that his heart could not have withstood the effects of the high-voltage electrical current for much longer.

Smith said that he had always wondered just how Sarge could have understood that his two human companions were being killed by the wire. "And even perceiving that, how did the old bulldog know that the wire must be cut in order to save their lives?"

• Chapter Six •

Is It Animal Intelligence or Animal Instinct?

There is considerable debate as to whether or not animals are born with certain genetically encoded information that tells them what to do and how to behave. For instance, the method in which mothers of various animal species raise their young or by what means they protect themselves and their young, how they select their young's diet, and how they determine what or who is the enemy are all things that we have come to believe animals don't need to be taught—or do they?

The assertion that animals possess certain innate instincts and don't need to learn the necessities of survival is simply not always true. Not all animals are born with the skills and knowledge essential to their preservation. Just watch newborn kittens or puppies. They are totally blind at birth, and remain so for about four to six weeks. They don't even know their own mother and they have no sense of direction. The fact is that most animals above the level of fish are quite helpless at first and need to be taught.

Baby elephants seem to have little idea of what purpose their trunk is to serve. Awkward and in their way, the trunk seems to be more of a hindrance than a helpful appendage until Mama elephant shows her young the many marvelous ways that trunk can be used.

Newborn ducks do not appear to know how to swallow their food. Baby chicks don't have the ability to distinguish their food from anything else, so their mother has to show them.

In the book *Animal Behavior* by Johann A. Loeser, we learn of an experiment with young moorhens that revealed some startling information. The baby moorhens who had not been shown by their mothers how to peck literally starved to death because they did not know how to get their food.

It does seem as though baby birds don't need to be taught how to sing, but in fact they do not sing very well unless they have had the benefit of being with their own species and listening to the song of their elders.

Parrots raised by humans and then released back into the wild have just enough of a difference in their call and song that they are rejected by the other birds almost as if they were an alien species.

Another example is the insects. It has been noted that their talents improve with practice. Young spiders begin weaving somewhat primitive webs. In the course of time they attain perfection in their geometric art.

Field mice improve their nest-building skills with age. They build better nests when they are older than they did as young mice.

Young birds need to be taught how to fly, and so do bats.

Many thousands of young sea lions and seals are drowned every year because they never learned how to swim. The mother has to take them under her flipper and instruct them.

• Chapter Seven •

Animal Education 101

Dolphins and whales need to be *taught* how to breathe. In the case of dolphins, either the mother or the dolphin midwives that assist in the birthing process nose the newborn baby calf to the surface of the water so it can take its first breath of air. If for any reason that doesn't happen, the baby whale or dolphin will drown, not realizing that it needs to breathe air, not water. Other dolphin midwives stay beneath the waves to care for the new mother.

This is interesting, as even humans need help to ensure that the first breath be taken. A baby is held upside-down, then given a little "pat" on its bottom, which brings about a cry and gasp for the very first breath of air.

Dolphin Midwives

Another fascinating development in birthing is a new process called *water birthing* . . . for humans. Dolphins make such good midwives for each other and are so loving and attentive that they are being recruited as midwives for human mothers! Some of our friends and associates have been studying this technique in the former Soviet Union for some ten or more years now, and are assisting some who wish to undergo this new method off the coast of California, in Hawaii, and in other locations.

French-born therapist Marie Helene Roussel says, "We already know that water birth is one of the most relaxing ways of having a baby." A developing fetus lives in water within the uterus for nine months; therefore, giving birth to the baby underwater is considered by many physicians to be less traumatic for the newborn baby and easier for the mother.

Roussel says, "We believe that being in contact with dolphins during labor can be therapeutic, relaxing, and help to make labor a painfree experience for the human mother."

Two mothers, one from New York and another from England, recently swam with dolphins and had the dolphins be the midwives in their babies' births in the Israeli resort city of Eilat, on the Red Sea lagoon. In these cases and many others all around the world, dolphins are teaching us humans!

Woodpecker Home Developers, Inc.

In the February, 1993, issue of *Wildbird* magazine, Dr. Evelyn Bull, Ph.D., and her husband, Michael Snyder, reported on their research with pileated woodpeckers—the largest woodpecker in North America.

Looking much like the cartoon character Woody the Woodpecker, pileated woodpeckers sport a crown of red feathers and are master carpenters. Whatever the reason, the woodpeckers have a brand new home and location every single year!

Many creatures take advantage of these prebuilt homes and move in when the woodpecker family moves out. Other species such as owls, bluebirds, flying squirrels, and wood rats in essence are "gifted" with a free home as each spring, pairs of pileateds excavate a new nest.

Mama and Papa woodpecker both share in the raising of their young. One will go in search of ants while the other baby-sits. When the nestlings have outgrown their need to be brooded, both Ma and Pa go for the groceries.

• Woodpecker School

In about four weeks, the fledglings attempt a limited flight, then follow their parents like shadows through the woods. If the brood is large, each parent will take some of the offspring for an individual training period; if the brood is small, both parents teach the young together. They spend at least several months teaching the young woodpeckers how to search for food—in other words, how to find invertebrates under logs and bark and in the interior of dead trees or logs.

• Self-Defense Classes

Mama and Papa woodpecker also instruct the young woodpeckers in the art of self-defense, teaching them how to escape their predators—chiefly hawks. The researchers reported that the maneuvers they observed being taught were fairly complex. They said the tactics seemed to be patterned after the squirrel's scurrying manner in order to outmaneuver the hawk. We do not know if the woodpeckers are astute observers, noticing the squirrels' success and wisely copying their moves, or just *how* they chose this technique, but in any event, it seems exceptionally clever!

• **Graduation**

In the fall, the young woodpeckers have learned their survival skills from Mom and Dad, and it's time to graduate and strike off on their own to apply their training. They go off in search of their own food . . . and perhaps to start the whole process again.

Animals Predict—Seers of the Future?

Many species of the animal kingdom seem to have a remarkable ability to predict the future . . . weather, that is. It is not known exactly how or why they know what weather patterns lie ahead in nature's path, but they do, and they take action in advance in order to be prepared for the season to come. In fact, animal predictions are very often more reliable than our own sophisticated weather forecasts!

Their uncanny accuracy in foretelling the future has long been observed and respected by Native Americans, who have a tradition of paying careful attention to animal behavior in order to know what the next season will bring and then follow the animals' example of how to prepare for it. Once again we find animals as teachers of humans!

Beavers and squirrels make special provisions according to the mildness or severity of the approaching season. If the weather is to be unusually inclement, the squirrel will be sure to store an abundance of food.

Crocodiles can predict the future level of the water line where they lay their eggs. Somehow they know *exactly* what will be the high-water line of the Nile. When the crocodiles lay their eggs to hatch, they do so at the exact point the water level will end up! They do this even if there is a radical change from high to low, or low to high. The water level frequently varies enormously, making this amazing skill of seeing into the future even more astounding. Many ancients observed the crocodile's accuracy and reacted accordingly. Even a crocodile can teach us a little something about life!

• Chapter Eight •

Can Animals Think?

You may be wondering by now how we can presuppose what an animal is thinking or . . . is this even possible?

According to the June, 1994, issue of *Omni* magazine, there is new research on mind reading and how the brain may interpret the intentions of others, which might give us some clues.

Nothing is more central to human thinking than the ability to interpret the thoughts of others or monitoring one's inner life, and this may apply to animals as well, according to scientists.

Leslie Brothers, a neuroscientist with the UCLA Brain Research Institute and the Sepulveda V.A. Medical Center, has come up with some interesting data.

Based on her research with macaque monkeys, Leslie said that the complexity of animal social life necessitates specific and changing responses to mates, offspring, leaders, rivals, in-group bullies, and allies. She states that all primates have developed very sophisticated means to decode or interpret the actions and activities of their fellows. "You have to be able to remember who's your friend. If you forgot someone wasn't nice to you—you would not survive very long," she says.

Brothers and her colleague Brian Ring have devised innovative experiments for the little-researched area of how the brain processes social information, and these experiments seem to indicate that some animals may have the ability to distinguish and process more data than we've thought they were capable of.

The researchers videotaped a group of outdoor monkeys as they groomed, ate, played, copulated, and slept. They showed close-ups of situations, of their interactions, of their individual eyes, ears, and so on, and transferred the 50,400 frames of footage onto a computer-controlled laser disc. In order to determine the way neural circuits generate macaque social behavior, they implanted tiny electrodes into single cells and parts of neuron ensembles in selected brain areas; then they recorded what neurons fired during what events when the monkeys were shown the movies of their filmed behavior.

Brothers found that certain *gestures* fired specific neurons. For example, during one episode when the observer monkey watched the film of a female monkey holding a piece of fruit as another monkey intently circled and approached her, a neuron fired strongly as the observer monkey watched this prelude to a handout. The neuron didn't fire during other situations, such as grooming or even when another monkey encircled a fellow monkey *without* fruit.

Brothers concluded that the data recorded from the electrodes was from the amygdala—areas of the brain central to processing emotions but with extensive pathways to the limbic and cortical regions—and that the amygdala are unifiers in a network for social cognition of converging pathways, sort of a "Times Square" of the brain. Other researchers have found specific socially responsive neurons in these areas of the brain as well.

Brothers also ascertained that social events may have privileged access to both motivational states and memory coding, forging an intimate link between emotions, memory, *and* perception. She says the emotional component *must* be present for the social information to have meaning.

This research opens up many doors to further research—not only on animal intelligence but animal emotions!

Recently, UCLA colleagues teamed with Brothers to continue the research with epileptic patients scheduled for surgery. The same areas of the brain are hooked up with electrodes but with a slightly different purpose—to track epileptic seizures. The patient watches a movie filled with emotional images in order to track neural activity during specific scenes and at the same time tell Brothers, who is a psychiatrist by training, *what* they're feeling at the same time as they reflect on their experiences.

Perhaps some day a mutual language, such as sign language, which some monkeys have learned to communicate with humans, will enable more two-way communication and understanding with the animals!

• Chapter Nine •

Innovative Animals

We have seen that the old adage "you can't teach an old dog new tricks" is not necessarily so, but how *do* animals learn? Do they have customs or rituals that are based on social learning? Are they capable of thinking or inventing?

The inventive process has generally been reserved for humankind ... or so we thought. Animals have not been regarded as capable of creating innovative discoveries or concepts of their own.

Even though we'll read about an elephant and a dolphin who paint in a later chapter, to date there hasn't been a genius composer, researcher, scientist, or artist such as Rembrandt or Picasso who has surfaced among the animal kingdom. However, information is amassing that changes entirely the way we view animals.

Recent research reveals animals to be capable of coming up with *new* ideas of their own that have not been taught to them by humans and cannot be attributed to instinct. Some of this same data has many broad and far-reaching implications that significantly alter our concept of the learning process—and in fact, of the very nature of life itself!

In 1952, on the island of Koshima, a group of scientists from the Primate Research Institute of Kyoto University in Japan were studying the behavior of Japanese macaque monkeys. They noted that cultural differences occur within the same breed that live in different regions. For instance, the macaques that live in Takasaki-yama throw away the hard stonelike pit found inside the fruit they eat from the muku tree, whereas the macaques from a different region of Arashi-yama break it with their teeth and eat the pulpy inside of the pit.

This might seem like an insignificant difference, you might be thinking. It could be likened to the difference between an Italian who eats spaghetti by twirling it around a fork, then guides it to his mouth with a spoon, and an Italian who cuts spaghetti with a fork and knife into more manageable bite-size portions. Although it would not matter in the least to most of us how one eats spaghetti, believe it or not, many Italians see a great deal of importance in this issue. Our daughter Kari, who married an Italian and has lived in Italy for many years now, tells us this is a very significant issue there, and there is a "right" way and a "wrong" way to eat spaghetti, depending on where you live, and a great many arguments spring from it!

This is important to us in this book, because researching these types of differences is what led to some incredible discoveries. In an effort to determine how behavior changes, spreads, or becomes indoctrinated in a species, a group of scientists put sweet potatoes on the beach, on the island of Koshima, in hopes of attracting monkeys near the shore for closer and easier observation.

The scientists observed that the monkeys seemed to really like raw sweet potatoes, but they did *not* like sweet potatoes covered with sand, which these were, of course, because they were on the beach, so the sweet potatoes were not being eaten very rapidly.

Not interfering, the scientists simply observed how the monkeys would deal with this. The macaques might attempt to eat a sweet potato many times, or even try others to see if they were different, only to find the gritty sand or dirt so distasteful that they'd lose interest.

Then all of a sudden one day, a young eighteen-month-old female macaque the scientists had named Imo found she could solve the dilemma of the dirty sweet potatoes by washing them in a nearby stream. Imo taught her discovery to her mother, then to her playmates, who also taught their own mothers.

Soon, over a process of time (between 1952 to 1958), and right before the scientists' very eyes, *all* of the young monkeys had learned this procedure of washing the grit and dirt off their sweet potatoes—they had learned that this process would make the sweet potatoes palatable.

The adult monkeys who did not learn from their children did not bother to wash the sweet potatoes; some of them even went ahead and ate them dirty.

Something mysterious occurred on one particular day, which has since come to be known as the "hundredth monkey phenomenon" (or syndrome). In the autumn of 1958, a certain number of Koshima monkeys were washing sweet potatoes—the exact number is not known. Then, just as if some magical number had been reached ... such as the *100th monkey* joining in to wash its sweet potato, almost all the monkeys, old and young, were washing their sweet potatoes.

The strangest thing is that *simultaneously*, colonies of monkeys on other islands, and even the mainland troop of monkeys at Takasaki-yama, began washing their sweet potatoes.

It was magical and mystifying—almost as though a mass demonstration had taken place on some huge movie screen that was seen by all monkeys in separate places! How could this happen?

Scientists speculate that perhaps when a certain critical number within a species achieves an awareness of something, this new awareness may then be communicated from mind to mind through the ethers.

The exact number may vary greatly for different concepts. In other words, if only a limited number of people or animals know of a new way, it might remain localized, and remain as the consciousness or property of a particular group.

But scientists say that there is perhaps a point at which if just one more person, animal, or living thing tunes in to a new awareness, a "field of thought energy" may occur that allows this awareness to reach everyone!

In fact, *all living things may communicate this way as well!* It has been proven that if one Dutch elm tree, for example, on one particular block has contracted Dutch elm disease, then other Dutch elm trees in the area (even blocks away) put out a defense-system alert by releasing a certain chemical to the leaves. If a certain number of trees respond to the signal and release their own protective chemical, then most trees will *not* get the disease.

If for some reason the trees pick up a stronger "sick signal" of the diseased tree (or trees)—without getting its immune system's protective chemical released to the leaves—then most likely that tree and a whole lot of others, perhaps even *all* of them in the area, will probably get the Dutch elm disease, and die.

• Chapter Ten •

Animals and "Mothering"

I s "mothering" an instinct that comes alive with hormonal changes accompanying the birth of new life, or is it instinctual or possibly an aspect of compassion or nurturing? Research into animal instinct and intelligence having to do with the care of the young have brought about some fascinating results.

We find it intriguing that stories seem to abound about animals that assist others of their own kind, but *not* so well known are cases of observances of animals helping *another* species, which was revealed by the same research.

One naturalist gave a chicken hen twenty-one guinea fowl eggs. At first it appeared the chicken didn't even notice that the eggs were not hers, because she treated them as though they were, even though they were quite different in appearance.

Then a surprise ... not even when the eggs hatched did Mama chicken show a difference in her behavior to the birds of a different feather. Somehow, Mama chicken turned out to have known all along that her "special" babies needed something different, something other than the normal food that a chicken eats.

To ensure that the babies would not starve (if they were ignored by the mother and treated as babies who weren't hers), the naturalist had set out mash for the little ones.

But Mama chicken scratched in some ants' nests until she exposed the pupae, which is the natural food source for guinea fowl babies! How could the chicken possibly have known what guinea fowl babies ate? Did this show some kind of intelligence . . . some kind of communication between the guinea fowl babies and the chicken mama?

If the chicken had been following natural instinct alone, researchers thought it would have been likely that she would have simply abandoned the babies, realizing they were not hers. How Mama chicken knew what to do, and why she nurtured them as her own babies, we do not know—but one thing is for certain; we are told that the adopted babies lapped up the ant eggs, and seemed to treat Mama chicken as if she were Mama guinea hen!

In another case, a researcher replaced a chicken mom's eggs with *duck* eggs. Once again, the response startled the researchers with the love the chicken showed to the "ugly ducklings" . . . as if they were her very own baby chicks.

When it came time, Mama chicken walked over to a plank, crossed a stream, and clucked at the adopted babies to follow her—inviting them into the water.

We all know chickens don't swim; but how did this mama chicken know "her" babies were ducks who did swim?!

This leads to further thoughts for us to ponder. In situations in their natural habitat, how do herds of vast numbers of cattle, cows, and elephants, identify one another—how would a mama know which baby is hers? There might be hundreds of baby cows; so how can the mama know which one is her baby?

In farming or cattle raising, where selective breeding is common, the calves may all look fairly similar, if not alike. In some cases, even the coloration would be nearly identical. To our human eye, the babies might all look the same; so is there a difference in the tone of their bellow and call that distinguishes them from another, or some other unknown factor?

Pulitzer Prize nominee John Robbins, in his book *Diet for a New America*, has done much to change the thinking of many who thought human beings the center of the universe.

Robbins recounts the story of one cow mother who was missing her calf. It seems that in 1953, a neighbor accused Mike Perkins of stealing his calf and then branding it with his own ranch's insignia.

The case was taken to court. The judge asked Perkins to bring all of his calves into the courtroom and for Perkins (the accused) to bring in the mama cow of the alleged stolen baby.

As soon as Mama cow arrived in the court, she began calling loudly. One by one the mama cow went over the line of calves, finally singling out one calf in particular. She licked this baby over and over again in the same spot ... right on the hip where the *P* was, Perkins' brand!

This motherly show of affection was enough for the judge to pronounce Perkins guilty and to return the calf to Mama cow and his neighbor.

"Many animals have a deep capacity to feel love and compassion, fear and grief," says Dr. Stephen Kritsick, staff veterinarian for the Humane Society of the United

States. "Animals often have very caring and enduring relationships with each other. In this they are more similar to us than we realize," he says.

"Animal mothers generally have strong maternal instincts to care [for] and protect their young," the doctor continues. It has even been noted by many that animal mothers often *surpass* human mothers in their selflessness and courage and in the intelligent ways they raise their young.

Dr. Mavis Newell, a psychologist and lecturer for The Study of Human Behavior in Canberra, Australia, declares, "As a species, we humans have much to learn from Mother Nature's other creatures about maternal love and dedication." Newell emphasizes that in the den or nest of a wild animal, we would not find such a thing as a battered or abused newborn.

Dr. Robin Fox, a noted animal behaviorist and vice-president of the Humane Society of the United States, echoes Dr. Newell's observations. Dr. Fox definitively expresses that there are many examples of extraordinary behavior in the animal world that definitely represent maternal love and simply *"cannot be a purely mechanical instinct."*

The following story illustrates, to us, extraordinary behavior . . . the sense of fairness and cooperation between cow mamas. See if you think it shows some kind of intelligence to be so "thoughtful."

Give Mama a Break!

A number of cattle breeders have told us stories over the years, about the special connection they observed, that existed between mother cows and their calves. This can make it very difficult at times for a breeder to separate them, which is inevitable, when they are sold. The following anecdote illustrates the essence of many of them.

A cow breeder from Iowa told us he was convinced that cows seem to have a wonderful cooperative system of baby-sitting for one another to ensure that all the mama cows get a well-deserved break.

He noticed that at nine o'clock in the morning, fifteen of his mama cows would methodically go off into the distant pasture to munch on grass or just lie around—as if enjoying some relaxing moments *without* their offspring. Remaining behind would be three of the mama cows with all of the baby calves.

Each cow "nanny" would be surrounded by five or six calves who were usually playfully frolicking around her. A few of the calves might be sitting or lying down, but no matter what they were doing, they would all be within 50 feet of her.

Every five to ten seconds, the "calf-sitter" would turn her head from side to side to keep a watchful eye out for the babies, and to be sure that there was no threat to them.

Around noon, the fifteen mama cows would come back from their outing. They would be with their calves until about four o'clock, then they would take off again for an afternoon break.

Although this would be a "typical" schedule, breeders and farmers have noted that the exact hours might vary, but that the cows always seemed fair, rotating the baby-sitting roles so that each cow mama would get a break.

The role of looking after the babies is taken so seriously that if the calves are hungry while their moms are on a break, the baby-sitting cows act as surrogate mothers, allowing the nurslings to feed from their nipples.

Young calves can be very playful and frisky, but if one of them should get a little too rambunctious or get out of line, the "calf-sitters" really put their foot down—literally! They stomp their feet *hard*, then bellow out a loud "moo" in a particular tone that as much as says to the calves, BEHAVE!

Dolphins and whales exhibit a most unusual sense of cooperation . . . as do elephants! We mentioned that dolphins need to be taught how to breathe; and explored how they are midwives, helping one another during the birthing process; well, dolphins and whales aren't alone in acting as midwives for each other in the birthing and protection of their newborns. Dr. Fox explains that female elephants will serve as midwives for one another, particularly older, experienced ones for the younger ones. The experienced elephants will help the newborn stand up by nudging and protecting it; then they will usually assist the mama elephant in getting rid of the placental tissues.

Most animal mothers will defend their young against attack or predators. Birds will often fake a broken wing in order to lure a predator away from their young. Even the wildebeest mother will rigorously defend her young from a major predator. Against all odds, she'll defend her young ones even if there is a whole pack of hungry hyenas after them. If she were following instinct alone, she'd turn and run to protect her own life in the survival of the fittest.

The abilities to *care, love, nurture,* and *protect* are generally attributed only to humans. To illustrate how false that is, Dr. Fox tells of a remarkable case that occurred in England:

Both a dairy cow and her young calf had been sold at market. The calf was taken to a farm seven miles away from where Mama cow would be. Mama cow was not going to stand for this separation from her calf; so, in spite of the 7-mile journey over a terrain completely unfamiliar to her, she made her trek to find her baby.

The very next day, the mama cow was found trying to batter her way into the enclosure where the calf was being kept. "There seems most definitely to be some kind of psychic maternal bond between this cow and her offspring," Dr. Fox says.

• Chapter Eleven •

Animals, Death, and Mourning

Another instinct that animals seem to have naturally, just as we do, is that of grief. It is only in recent years that we humans have taken seriously our own need to express grief at appropriate times and understand that there is an actual *grieving process* of various stages that we all go through when a loved one passes on. The recognition of this process in humans is quite progressive, and it has been the norm in the past not to recognize that animals even had emotions.

Animals seem to possess a high degree of awareness, almost as if they have a sixth sense, about their own impending death. When that time arrives for them, they exhibit behavior accordingly—setting themselves apart from the rest of the pack or herd.

The day after a terrible circus fire, a United Press dispatch from Hartford told of the surviving animals' reaction to the tragedy. The loss of their fellow animal circus performers was met with obvious signs of grief. Gargantua the gorilla was said to be wailing unceasingly. The lion refused to eat. The tiger crouched in a corner in its cage and meowed in an agonizing, mournful litany. One of the circus personnel told the reporter that it was obvious that the animals knew when death was near.

In the wild, researchers have been able to observe certain behaviors of animals who seem to sense when their demise is near. The wolf, for example, will leave the others and find a quiet place to spend his last hours in total solitude. An elephant in the wild that is about to die will leave the herd as it sets out to find a private graveyard.

The swan is a silent bird in life, seldom making a sound until it is about to die, then it performs a final dying serenade, hence the expression "swan song" to designate someone's final purposeful act.

Another little-known observance of animal behavior are those cases where animals exact retribution for an injury or harm caused to its beloved mates or offspring. This has been noted by Eric Daglish, a researcher and author in his *The Life Story of Beasts* (New York: William Morrow and Company), written in 1931, that bears will travel "scores of miles, if need be, to avenge the loss of their young."

Daglish also told of the vendetta of seals if one of their pack has been hurt. He said that herds of seals will fall, "as if all part of one big seal body onto the foe responsible for the suffering of their comrade."

Heartwarming stories from many researchers are validating the nearly unvarying nature of the maternal attachment to beloved offspring, even if the infant has been stillborn or died from some cause soon after birth.

Eric Daglish noted that female baboons cling to their dead babies long after they are dead. The mother clutches the dead infant's body to her and will not give it up. She'll carry it with her and give it the same attention that a live newborn needs to survive.

The mother baboon will make pathetic attempts, in

vain, to feed and even play with her newborn. It's an extremely sad and pitiful thing to behold. It's almost as if the mother believes that if she carries it long enough and tries hard enough to feed it and give it love and attention that the baby will miraculously come back to life.

In the past, it was generally believed that grieving animal mothers might not have the intelligence to perceive the death of their offspring. Some recent observations are changing such beliefs, and there are accounts in which an animal mother will assist in the death of her infant, rather than see it suffer an injury or allow it to be captured.

An old clipping from the *Chicago Sun* newspaper, May 1, 1944, told of a lioness who destroyed her offspring rather than allow them to be captured by humans who were pursuing them.

The article referred to Mr. Ernest Thompson Seton, a popular author of the early 1900s as the source of the information. Seton observed, studied and wrote about nature stories that gave evidence of a high degree of "moral order" in the animal kingdom. Sincere in his pursuit, Seton claimed to have personally witnessed this account.

Seton tells of a lioness who brought her cub a piece of poisoned bait so that it would die in the trap in which it had been ensnared rather then permit it to end up in the hands of the humans who had set the snare.

When tuna fisherman capture dolphin babies in their nets along with the tuna they are fishing for, the mama dolphins will often jump in the net to be with their offspring even though it will cost them their lives.

• Chapter Twelve •

Animals That Care for and Mother Humans!

Friend, a golden retriever, serves as arms, legs, eyes, and ears for her owner, Linda Storey, who suffers from multiple sclerosis and is confined to a wheelchair.

In addition to performing all the duties of a house-maid, Friend did such a wonderful job fulfilling the role of nanny to Linda's five-year-old daughter, Jennifer, that the Storeys decided to have a second child. When baby Matthew arrived in the household, Friend had no trouble adjusting to her new responsibility.

Linda Storey has lost the use of her legs and cannot walk. She has the full use of only one arm, so Friend must supplement her disabilities with a willing paw or two around the house. The Storeys, who reside in Englewood, Colorado, consider Friend a "godsend."

Ken Storey commented that it is a great relief to know that if there is ever an emergency at home while he is at work, Friend will be there to place the telephone in Linda's hand.

Quadriplegic Robert Foster calls his capuchin monkey his baby, but in fact this tiny, twelve-year-old housemaid cares for her incapacitated master.

Robert has been able to move only his head and shoulders since he was an eighteen-year-old survivor of an automobile accident. Now in his mid-thirties, the Boston native relies on his magic monkey to assist him in living as normal a life as possible.

Although Robert would undoubtedly insist that his capuchin should bear the name of Angel, the folks at Capuchins Helping Hands who trained her handed her the monicker of Hellion.

Well, what's in a name? Helpful Hellion is as accomplished a nursemaid as any human might be. And she has infinitely more patience.

Robert's wheelchair is equipped with a chin control that permits him to point at any object that he might wish Hellion to pick up for him. However, if the mechanism moves just two inches to one side, it can immobilize his head. One of his tiny nursemaid's jobs is to be ever on the alert to push the chin control back into place.

Hellion scampers across the floor to the refrigerator, removes a large plastic container, then carries it to the table, where she carefully spoon-feeds Robert his meal. When her master indicates that he has had enough, Hellion returns the leftovers to the refrigerator.

Robert and Hellion have two other roommates who could certainly be a bit more fastidious. It seems that Robert's two cats sometimes scatter their kitty litter beyond the confines of their basket, and Hellion is forced to clean up the mess with the carpet sweeper.

While there are countless instances in which animals have been trained to become highly efficient nursemaids for their human owners, there also exist numerous documented accounts of those remarkable instances in which pets or undomesticated animals have assumed the role of surrogate parents to human children left unattended or somehow appointed to their care.

Nearly all of us are familiar with the fictional character of Mowgli, the Indian boy raised by wolves in Rudyard Kipling's *The Jungle Book*, and of Edgar Rice Burroughs' Tarzan of the Apes, who has become one of the most famous creations of the human imagination in the world.

Because of the popularity of such tales, it becomes difficult to convince the modern skeptic that such stories of animals caring for and rearing human children can be other than fiction.

In the fall of 1992, Iowa farmer Joe Chilton stopped by a neighbor's place to leave a basket of tomatoes from his garden. Perhaps this might seem rather odd if you are a city person, but in small Midwestern towns this is a very common and neighborly thing to do. In fact, when we moved back to Iowa, the first time the plumber-electrician came for repairs, he brought with him a shopping bag full of sweet corn and tomatoes from his backyard garden.

It was also not unusual to hear the dogs barking in the neighborhood, but this time Chilton noticed one particular bark with a peculiar pitch to it.

When his curiosity compelled him to investigate, he was shocked to find a young boy among the dog pack, howling, growling, and barking like the others.

Chilton could only conclude that the boy was his neighbors' son, the lad that had many years earlier dropped out of sight.

Chilton's wife had once baby-sat for the boy, and they knew that the child was hyperactive. When he entered his "terrible twos," the kid's mother was fit to be tied.

Later, whenever Chilton would inquire about the lad, he would be given one story after another to explain away his mysterious disappearance. Now it appeared, as terrible as it sounds, that for *seven years*, the little boy had been made to live with the dogs in the kennel.

Robert Lake, social services supervisor, classified the plight of the "dog-boy" as "absolutely the most horrible case of emotional abuse" that he had ever seen.

When social workers arrived to remove the boy from the doghouse on the farm near Hull, Iowa, he barked at them, growled, and tried to bite them.

Therapists who later sought to analyze the nine-year-old noted that he habitually circled chairs before sitting down and snapped at people whenever he was under stress.

"We can only assume the boy's bizarre behavior was caused by his long association with animals," Robert Lake commented.

The boy is currently undergoing intensive therapy, and mental health personnel hold out hope that he will eventually recover from his seven-year ordeal in his parents' kennel. Although they realize that such a transition will take time, they optimistically foresee the day when he will once again adjust to life as a human.

• Chapter Thirteen •

The Mystery of Lost Animals Who Find Their Way Home—Even to Homes Where They Have Never Been

Princess the Calico Cat's 100-Mile Odyssey

Ronald and Peggy Keaton of Grand Rapids, Michigan, made no secret of the fact that their whole family pampered Princess, their beautiful calico cat. In fact, the feline had been so sheltered that she had only been out of the house once in her three-year life.

And then, in June of 1991, Mrs. Keaton's mother, who lived in Toledo, Ohio, became ill, and Peggy left at once with their four-year-old son and two-year-old daughter to be at the ailing woman's side.

A few days later, Ronald Keaton and their six-year-old daughter, Stacy, crawled into the van with Princess to drive to Toledo. Although he knew the trip might be difficult for their coddled cat, Keaton felt that he could not risk leaving her home alone.

And then somewhere between Grand Rapids and Toledo, Princess vanished.

Keaton had made a pit stop at a highway rest area about 100 miles from home. He was certain Princess was still in the van at that time, because he distinctly remembered that he had difficulty getting back in the van because she was resting against the window on the driver's side. He further recalled that Stacy had crawled in first and moved Princess out of his way. Both he and his daughter assumed that the cat then moved to the back of the van to find a comfortable spot to take a nap.

Keaton drove straight through to his mother-in-law's home in Toledo. He did not make another stop, so no one discovered that Princess had disappeared until they were unpacking the van.

The three children were distraught; and since all of the Keatons were well aware of the delicate nature of their pampered pussy cat, they forced themselves to accept the grim reality that Princess did not have the slightest chance of surviving all by herself in the cruel world.

In the next few days, Peggy and Ronald focused their concern on the needs of Peggy's ailing mother. And then one night one of their neighbors back in Grand Rapids telephoned the Keatons to inform them that Princess was sitting on the doorstep of their home, impatiently awaiting their return.

Somehow, their pampered, precious Princess had managed to walk back to Grand Rapids from the rest stop 100 miles away and return to the correct house.

Apparently, their darling calico was made of much sterner stuff than any member of the Keaton family had been willing to acknowledge.

When it comes to cats who have returned home under miraculous circumstances, Princess' odyssey hardly holds the record.

Li-Ping's Journey from Ohio to Florida

In April of 1955, when Vivian Allgood, a registered nurse, moved from Sandusky, Ohio, to Orlando, Florida, she was forced to leave her beloved cat, Li-Ping, behind in the care of a sister.

Months later, to Ms. Allgood's total astonishment, who should walk up to her door but Li-Ping! The bedraggled cat had somehow managed to travel hundreds of completely unfamiliar miles to find his mistress in a state, neighborhood, and home that he had *never* been to and never seen. Ohio to Florida is an extremely long trip, even by car—so it is astounding to think that a pet that has no road map, no ability to read, no ability to understand road signs or to ask for directions could accomplish such a feat on little cat feet! How do you suppose this is possible?

Rusty the Cat Sets Speed Record for Hiking 1,000 Miles in Eighty-Three Days!

Another astounding cat journey occurred in 1949, when a Chicago cat named Rusty established the fastest feline travel time on record. Separated from his family while they were vacationing in Boston, this incredible cat somehow managed to find his way back home to Chicago.

Experts who have studied this homing-cat record have concluded that Rusty somehow must have found a way to hitch rides on trains, trucks, and automobiles in order to cover the nearly 1,000 miles in eighty-three days.

Tom the Cat Travels 2,500 Miles!

The long-distance record for cats was set by Tom, who got left behind in St. Petersburg, Florida, when his owners Mr. and Mrs. Charles B. Smith moved to San Gabriel, California, in 1949.

Although it took him two years and six weeks, in August of 1951 he staggered into the Smiths' yard in their new home—2,500 miles away.

This is even more astounding than the Rusty story. Tom traveled across the *entire* United States not knowing where his owners had moved! Somehow, obviously desperate to find them, he had some kind of built-in sense that not only located his masters . . . but their new house. Tom had found his way "home" to a home where he had never been!

Oscar the Beagle Makes His Way from New York to Indianapolis, Indiana

True to the classic "Lassie Come Home" tradition, dogs are no slackers when it comes to finding their way to their masters' old or new homes under conditions that can only be described as "impossible."

When the Hutchinson family moved from New York to Indianapolis in October of 1988, they left behind their beagle Oscar with a grandson who was extremely fond of the dog. Although four-year-old Oscar had never left the confines of the old neighborhood, he arrived at the Hutchinsons' new home in Indiana seven months later.

Lean and bedraggled, his foot pads raw and bloody, Oscar proved that he loved his owners far more than he esteemed the place where they had left him.

Joker the Cocker Spaniel Joins the Army to Find His Master

During World War II, Joker, a cocker spaniel, got left behind on the home front when his owner, army captain Stanley C. Raye, was shipped off to a remote island in the South Pacific.

Joker pined for his master for only two weeks before he somehow made his way to Oakland, California, and managed to get on board an army transport.

The skipper was about to order the stowaway mutt tossed overboard when a sympathetic major volunteered to look after him.

Although the transport made many stops to deliver various military goods to the army bases, Joker somehow seemed to know by sniffing the air at each island that his master wasn't there . . . not at *any* of them.

When the transport docked at one particular port of call in the South Pacific, Joker jumped ship and raced to the side of a most astonished captain Stanley C. Raye! How could Joker possibly have known where his owner had been shipped?

Since the dog had never been on board a ship in his life, how could he possibly have guessed what mode of transportation would take him to his owner?

Our friends among the traditional American Indians believe that all of life is unified. Rather than seeing themselves as having dominion over the beasts, birds, and fish, they perceive all life-forms as being interconnected. As we mentioned in Chapter 9—"Innovative Animals"—perhaps the 100th monkey phenomenon explains some part of the mystery of the connection of all life on a quantum physics level. *Perhaps* animals are more sensitive to the subtle energies that connects us all; thereby finding their way. What do you think?

Baby the Epileptic Cocker Spaniel Fights Near-Impossible Odds to Find Owner

Baby, a cocker spaniel–poodle mix who suffered from epileptic seizures, managed to find her way back to the John Donegan family of Addison, Illinois, on September 9, 1969, after having been dognapped and held for eight months.

To complicate matters for Baby, the Donegans had moved to Addison from Melrose Park, and the dog had first to find the trailer home of Mrs. Catherine Geitz, Mrs. Donegan's mother, to appeal for help.

Donegan theorized that the dognappers grew puzzled when Baby had one of her epileptic fits. They quite likely didn't understand what was happening and threw her out.

Mrs. Geitz lived more than 15 miles from the Donegans' new home, but Baby had visited "Grandma's" house with the family before she had been dognapped.

Mrs. Donegan said that Baby looked terrible when she finally found her way home: "Her nose was sunburned and swollen; her feet were raw; and two back teeth were broken. But it was our Baby! She still had her dog tags on. Now our family is back together again."

Skippy Escapes from Dognapper and Finds Way Home . . . 600 Miles!

Skippy was another dognapping victim who escaped from his captors. A few years ago, Skippy was snatched from his home in Mt. Clemens, Michigan; but he returned to his delighted owner six months later with a dog tag that had been issued in Fort Dodge, Iowa.

How had Skippy managed to find his way 600 miles

back home when he had never been out of Mt. Clemens before in his life?

How did *any* of the cats and dogs profiled above manage to accomplish what appears to be an almost supernatural ability to zero in on their human families wherever they might be?

Those stories in which a cat or dog finds its way *back* to an established and familiar home over hundreds of miles are remarkable enough, for these accounts seem to reveal some fantastically developed homing instinct.

But the reports of pets who have traversed unfamiliar and far-distant landscapes to locate their human families in new homes seem to defy all easy explanations.

Somehow the image of a pooch or a tabby hitchhiking with a map under its arm just doesn't seem to satisfy the reality of these extraordinary feats of seeking out lost and found human families.

Dr. Larry Dossey, a doctor of internal medicine with the Dallas Diagnostic Association and former chief of staff of Medical City Dallas Hospital, who has authored the fascinating *Recovering the Soul—A Scientific and Spiritual Search*, remarks that it would be difficult to convince millions of pet owners that they do not on occasion "communicate" with their dogs, cats, birds—or even their goldfish.

"Everyone," he comments, "has felt at one time or another on the same 'wavelength' with an animal."

• Chapter Fourteen •

Your Dog Can Be Your Doctor

Dogs Provide an Early Warning System Against Heart Attacks and Epileptic Seizures

In a recent study of the interaction of dogs with people prone to epileptic seizures, diabetic coma, and heart attacks, veterinary researcher Andrew Edney, D.V.M., states that dogs may provide a highly effective early warning system.

Edney carefully examined the accounts of 121 dogs who had allegedly given warning to their owners that a seizure or an attack was about to occur.

In certain instances, according to Ivor Smullen in the July 1993 issue of *Longevity* magazine, the dog began to bark, nuzzle, or jump up on the victim as much as forty-five minutes before the episode, "trying to get the victim to lie down and even herding him or her to safety or alerting others in the household."

Edney theorizes that someday dogs may be trained to

assist heart attack victims to recognize danger signals or to alert diabetics to the onset of a hypoglycemic coma. In his research, Edney found that collies and other "working" dogs, such as the German shepherd or the Labrador retriever. As we have already stated, these breeds are most commonly trained to lead the blind as Seeing Eye dogs and the like.

Exactly how a dog determines that his or her owner is about to be taken by an attack or seizure is a matter of speculation. There are many possible explanations as to what might cue a dog that something out of the normal is about to happen, such as: subtle changes in the owner's usual behavior, the release of a distinctive chemical or odor, and/or sudden alterations in the electrical or bioelectric field. Researchers are still attempting to discover and document these and other viable clues of the diagnostic dogs!

Ribbon Has Unerring Accuracy in Forecasting Her Owner's Seizures

Ribbon, the loyal companion of Dr. Elizabeth Rudy, has been forecasting the onset of her owner's epileptic seizures with unerring accuracy since 1983.

Dr. Rudy, a Seattle, Washington, veterinarian, said that she experiences about one seizure a month. If Ribbon is on a leash when she senses her owner's impending seizure, she will stop instantly and put her ears down. If the two of them are indoors, Ribbon will lick Dr. Rudy's hands, then sit staring at her or continue licking her hands.

Within a few minutes of Ribbon's alert, Dr. Rudy's own internal warning mechanism alerts her with the odor of burning flesh. For whatever reason, this lets her know that in less than a minute after such an inner manifestation, she will experience a loss of consciousness;

and even though she will soon regain control, she will still be slightly disoriented. Now, just to clarify, her flesh is *not* actually burning, but just as when we can sometimes "sense" things, she "senses" this type of smell.

Have you ever had a funny feeling that someone was staring at you, for instance, and you turn around just in time to catch someone either quickly turning his or her head away—or still looking at you? Or have you "sensed" that the phone was about to ring, and it did? Perhaps these remarkable animals have a highly developed form of the same kind of sensitivity.

Regina Berner, executive director of the Epilepsy Institute in New York, stated that she is aware of at least a dozen cases in which dogs alert their owners to the onset of an epileptic seizure. The Epilepsy Institute hopes to raise the necessary funds to be able to conduct a program that would match dogs with such talents with epileptics who fear unexpected seizures in inconvenient or dangerous places.

Sheba Gave Her Owner Relief from a Lifelong Nightmare

Because of the vigilance of her watchdog Sheba, Angie Barnum was able to graduate with honors from high school in Gig Harbor, Washington, to win medals at the Special Olympics, and to become a gymnastics coach.

Now in her early twenties, Angie, a victim of a partial complex multiple seizure disorder, a form of epilepsy, has suffered from violent seizures since the age of ten months. As she matured, she was forced to be confined to a wheelchair, for she could suffer as many as fifteen seizures a day.

In 1983, Angie received relief from her perpetual

nightmare when Sheba entered her life. The year-old German shepherd seemed to take at once to his special mission of protecting Angie and alerting her to the onset of her seizures.

According to Angie's parents, Pat and Orin Barnum, Sheba can sense an impending seizure even while their daughter is sleeping.

On one occasion that nearly brought terrible tragedy, Sheba awakened Mrs. Barnum and brought her to Angie's room, where she was frightened to discover that her daughter's heart and breathing had stopped. She immediately administered CPR and was able to restore Angie to life.

Due to Sheba's remarkable ability to detect the onslaught of her seizures, Angle was also restored to a normal social life. With Sheba at her side, she was able to go on dates, do volunteer work at the Humane Society, and, incredibly, even participate in sports.

Because Sheba was there with her, Angie was able to compete as a gymnast at the 1987 International Special Olympics, and she won a gold medal on the balance beam and took home three other bronze medals.

Medical experts theorize that Sheba may be able to sense the onset of her owner's seizures due to a drop in Angie's body temperature or a subtle chemical change in her body odor. Sheba becomes restless, then she'll position herself in front of Angie and force her to sit down so she won't fall.

Malignant Melanomas May Emit a Distinctive Odor to a Dog's Keen Sense of Smell

Just a few years ago, Bonita Whitfield, who lives near London, England, began to notice that whenever she was clad only in shorts or in her undies, Baby, her mixed-breed dog, would start to make a fuss, whining and attempting to bite her on the thigh.

Bonita was thoroughly puzzled by her dog's behavior, since he was normally very gentle and even-tempered; and she had scolded him dozens of times before she began to pay special attention to the fact that Baby seemed upset over one particular mole on the back of her thigh.

When she at last had the mole removed at King's College Hospital in London, she was notified that it was definitely a malignant melanoma, which, fortunately, the surgeons removed before it could spread.

Dr. Hywel Williams, a staff physician in the dermatology department at King's College, said that the mole would have appeared completely normal to a layperson's untrained eye. How Baby had acquired the medical knowledge to recognize a malignant melanoma remained a mystery. Perhaps Baby had saved his owner's life by possessing the ability to "sniff out" skin cancer.

Dr. Williams went on to theorize that melanomas may emit a distinctive odor that certain dogs are able to smell, and he told journalists that he planned to initiate a study to investigate such a hypothesis.

If the research proved successful, he speculated, there might well be a place for dogs in the screening process for malignant melanomas.

Owning a Pet Significantly Reduces the Risk of Heart Disease

A medical study of more than 5,000 patients conducted by Dr. Warwick Anderson of the Baker Medical Research Institute discovered that pet owners had significantly reduced levels of known risk factors for cardiovascular disease. As amazing as it may seem, people can reduce their cholesterol levels and lower their blood pressure simply by owning a pet.

Dr. Leo Bustad of the College of Veterinary Medicine at Washington State University has noted that the word about the contribution that a pet can make to a person's health has been spreading slowly but surely, in spite of resistance from certain scientists who refuse to view animals as having any significant contributions to make to human health.

Animal researchers have known for years that a dog's heart rate and blood pressure drop when it is being petted. Now science is proving that contact with pets accomplishes the same effects for their human masters. Petting your pooch relieves stress, which, in turn, alters body chemistry and slashes the risk of heart disease.

Dogs Make Magnificent Therapists in Cancer Units

Robin Tenny, director of the cancer unit at Desert Samaritan Hospital in Mesa, Arizona, has found that Buddy, a mutt that her husband, John, snatched from the jaws of death at the animal pound, has been working miracles in the lives of the cancer patients under her care. When Buddy enters a patient's room, he or she begins to glow with love and happiness.

Buddy had to pass rigorous tests before he could become one of an elite corps of 8,000 registered therapy dogs in the United States. Each pooch is insured for one million dollars and is issued a special health certificate. Therapy dogs get their teeth brushed, their ears cleaned, and their toenails snipped each week.

Owning a Pet Makes Senior Citizens Healthier and Happier

Dr. Erika Friedmann of Brooklyn College recently released the results of a survey of senior citizens, which concludes that those with pets were healthier and happier than those without fido or feline.

According to Dr. Friedmann, professor of Health and Nutrition Sciences, when people sit quietly in the presence of a friendly animal, their heart rate is lower. This is great news for people who suffer from high blood pressure, one of the leading causes of heart attack. Scientists have found evidence that contact with animals can also calm disturbed children, prompt uncommunicative people to converse, and increase a sick person's chances for survival.

A nationwide survey of 600 men and women over the age of fifty conducted by Strategic Directions Group of Minneapolis found that 43 percent of the interviewees owned a pet and 57 percent of that number stated that their pets were very important in their lives.

Experts interviewed for the University of Texas Lifetime Health Letter agree with such findings and add that spending time with a dog lowers blood pressure, eases depression, and stimulates the production of endorphins, the human body's natural tranquilizers.

Researchers at the University of Pennsylvania determined that elderly heart patients who kept pets lived much longer than those who had no animal to keep them company.

Pet Owners of Any Age Require Less Medical Attention

A report published in the *Journal of Personality and Social Psychology* stated that patients of any age who owned any type of pet made far fewer visits to the doctor.

Of all pet owners, those who kept dogs came out on top, requiring medical attention 21 percent less often than people who lived without a canine companion.

Dogs Help Women Lower Stress More Effectively than a Close Friend

Dr. Karen Allen, associate professor in the School of Medicine at the State University of New York at Buffalo, studied forty-five women who owned dogs and discovered that canines were able to help their owners deal better with stress than the comfort of a close friend.

In an experiment in which subjects were asked to perform tension-building arithmetic problems, Dr. Allen said, the presence of another person, even a close friend, did not help to reduce elevated levels of pressure, pulse rate, and palm sweating.

With a pet present, however, the participants' physical responses remained normal. "The ease with which the task was accomplished was much better with the dog present," Dr. Allen said.

The concept of animals making good companions for the sick is not actually a new one. It goes back at least as far as the 1790s when a Quaker retreat in York, England, encouraged patients to spend time with small animals.

Add all of this up and you might concur with Judith Siegel, professor of Public Health at University of California at Los Angeles, (UCLA) that "pet ownership might provide a new form of low-cost health intervention."

Woman's Best Friend

In the July-August 1994 issue of *Modern Maturity* magazine, an article entitled "Woman's Best Friend" gives equal status to the "man's best friend" idea. Ken Wibecan tells of a "working dog" who looks like any other playful, lovable Labrador retriever. But in essence, Gally is Ms. Snyder's eyes and security.

Snyder told Wibecan that as her vision faded, she lost her waitressing job. Finding herself unable to go out much because of her loss of sight, she went to the Guide Dog Foundation for the Blind in Smithtown, New York.

The newfound freedom and security that Ms. Snyder gained enable her to go places with her Seeing Eye dog and have a sense of independence. She no longer has to depend totally on her husband or daughters to take her places. An irony that she joked about was how all of her life she loved and cared for animals, but never did she think one would take care of her!

Sole Caretaker

There are of course many such stories of men, women, and children who are cared for by "working" dogs. In many cases, especially of the elderly, there may be no family or friends there at all. In these situations, the working dog not only becomes the seeing eyes of its master and the best friend but often the total caregiver, to the extent of even delivering groceries, bills, Braille books, and so on to and from their respective places.

• Chapter Fifteen •

Superdogs to the Rescue!

The Dog He Didn't Want in His House Saved His Life

Nora Martyniak of Lakeville, Massachusetts, was seeing a guest to the door on a snowy evening in December 1992 when she heard the new dog, Tina, barking loudly from her husband's den.

Perhaps her greatest worry as she started toward the den to investigate what was happening was her concern that her forty-seven-year-old husband, Steve, was having it out with Tina.

Nora had argued with Steve for days to let her keep the sad-eyed mutt that kept hanging around her office. While he had been vehemently opposed to her bringing the dog home, she had just as strongly felt some kind of peculiar compulsion to adopt the pooch.

And now, after Tina had been a resident of their home for only a few days, Nora was fearful that the relationship was coming to a stormy end. She knew that Steve had just finished shoveling snow from the walk and had gone back to his study to rest. If Tina was disturbing him with her noisy barking, Nora knew that the little dog would soon be given her walking papers.

But when she entered Steve's study, she found the barking dog perched atop his chest, apparently trying desperately to convey the message that the man of the house was terribly ill.

Nora pushed Tina off and was horrified to see that his face was blue and that he seemed to have stopped breathing.

Convinced that Steve had died, she felt herself slipping into hysteria and helplessness. "Oh, my God," she screamed aloud. "He's dead!"

But Tina was not about to give up. She continued to jump at Steve's chest, as if trying to jolt his heart back into pumping life through his body.

At the same time, Nora heard an inner voice telling her that if she did not act quickly, her husband really would be dead. She pushed Tina away once again and began to pound on his chest.

Miraculously, he began breathing.

When Steve returned from five days of observation in the hospital, he set about spoiling Tina on a regular basis. He was no longer the slightest bit upset with his wife for having brought home the dog who saved his life.

And Nora suspects that there may well have been some greater plan at work when she felt the strange compulsion to adopt Tina.

Sparky Dragged His Master a Quarter of a Mile to Safety

On January 24, 1992, fifty-one-year-old Bo Culbertson, a former football coach from Tullahoma, Tennessee, was heading home from his morning walk accompanied by Sparky, his golden Labrador. Suddenly, Culbertson felt very ill. At first he thought he might just need to rest a bit, but then he began to feel chest pains and a tightness spreading across his left shoulder.

While his vision was slipping into blackness, he managed to get his left hand under Sparky's choke collar. The last thing that he remembered before he lost consciousness was Sparky licking his face.

Sparky continued to head home as usual, with his 237-pound owner—only this time, he was pulling his master behind him! The golden Labrador managed to tug and pull Culbertson a quarter of a mile to deliver him to the front door.

Mrs. Culbertson was shocked when she opened the door to view her unconscious husband with his left hand under Sparky's collar. Although she could see that Bo was still alive, one look at the bluish color of his face advised her that death might not be far away.

After she had rushed her husband to the local hospital, medical personnel stabilized him, then transferred him to larger facilities in Nashville, where Bo Culbertson underwent triple bypass surgery.

Later, one of the doctors stated that Sparky had saved Culbertson's life in two ways: first, by dragging him home so he would receive proper care as soon as possible; and second, the very act of tugging, pulling, and twisting him over rough terrain had continued to force blood into his heart.

Once out of danger, Culbertson remarked that Sparky was much more than a quick-thinking dog—he was a close friend.

Hotai the Chow Saved His Owner from Death by Fire

In January 1993, Hotai, a ten-week-old chow puppy jumped onto Alma Hudson's bed and began licking her face. The sixty-one-year-old San Antonio woman brushed him off and went back to sleep. It was not quite dawn, and she certainly was not in the mood to play with her new pup.

But Hotai began to pull at the covers, determined to wake his mistress. Alma sat up, wondering what on earth had possessed Hotai. He have never behaved in such a manner before.

That was when she saw at last the clouds of smoke billowing into the bedroom.

She crossed the room to wake her friend, Thomas Hotman, who was still sleeping soundly. Explaining that the house seemed to be on fire, she urged him to go investigate.

Hotman found his way through the smoke-filled upstairs hallway, then made his way down the stairs where he located a smoldering chair and couch. He started to beat out the fire with a rug, but the flames scattered to the carpet and soon raged out of control.

Recognizing that he had lost the battle to quench the fire, Hotman attempted to return upstairs to rescue his companion; but he was forced back by the flames, smoke, and intense heat.

Remembering the balcony off the master bedroom, Hotman ran outside and got a ladder to lean against the side of the house. Alma was there, holding Hotai in her arms.

Without hesitation, she threw the puppy into Hotman's waiting arms; then once Hotai was on the ground, she descended as quickly as possible down the ladder.

Afraid of heights, Alma found the descent frightening, but she realized that she and Hotman were lucky to be alive.

She also knew that they owed their lives to the pint-sized puppy who wouldn't stop licking her face or tugging at the covers until she was wide awake.

Toya Braved Mountains and Snowdrifts to Bring Help to Her Injured Owner

Sedrup Ole Hanssen had always considered Toya, his four-year-old Labrador–German shepherd mix, to be his best friend; and in November of 1992, she was able to prove it by saving his life.

Hanssen, fifty-two, his son Olav, twenty-three, and a friend had set out early in the morning on a cross-country ski trip across the snowy mountain trails of the Arctic Circle region north of their home in Vagehamm, Norway.

By noon, Olav and his friend wished to return home, but Hanssen and Toya wanted to remain longer to enjoy the stark beauty of the area.

Not long after his son left them, however, Hanssen fell as he was speeding down a steep slope and dislocated his kneecap. Hanssen found that he could not stand up. And as he was forced to remain motionless, he felt the terrible Arctic cold begin to penetrate his ski clothes. He knew that he could not last long in the sub-zero temperature.

Toya stood by his side, whimpering her concern. She knew that her owner was in serious trouble—and perhaps both human and canine realized at the same moment that she was his only chance to get home alive.

Hanssen tucked his ski cap under Toya's collar and told her to get Olav.

Toya barked and set off at a trot. Hanssen knew that the big dog would have to battle increasing cold, struggle through snowdrifts up to her ears, and run up a steep mountain slope. But the Norwegian had no doubt that his faithful dog would fulfill her mission.

Two miles of rough terrain later, Toya was within sight of Olav and his friend, and she began to bark an alarm. When the two young men saw Hanssen's ski cap under her collar, they knew she had been sent to get their help.

Toya took only a moment or two to catch her breath, and then she was off on the return trip, racing ahead of the men on their cross-country skis.

The doctor who later treated Hanssen's injured knee said that the skier would not have lasted another hour in the frigid Arctic weather.

Hanssen knew that his best friend would not have let him down.

The Amazing German Shepherds of the American Rescue Dog Association

Penny Sullivan, president of the American Rescue Dog Association (ARDA), is justifiably proud of the elite pack of fifty German shepherds—all specially trained to track down people by following scent trails in the air instead of on the ground.

As incredible as it may seem, by the fall of 1991, the dogs of ARDA had solved 1,425 of the 1,500 missing persons cases to which they had been assigned. That's nine out of ten missing men and women located by the German shepherds, a remarkable 95 percent success rate.

Perhaps equally remarkable is the fact that the superdogs work for nothing. ARDA's handlers are all volunteers who provide their dogs' tracking services without charge to law enforcement and rescue agencies throughout the country. The shepherds search for people in mudslides, landfills, trash piles, and buildings destroyed by fire.

ARDA chooses to work with German shepherds because the big dogs are tough and intelligent.

Sullivan said that the dogs undergo an entire year of rigorous training, learning to "air-scent," rather than to sniff the ground for clues to the whereabouts of a missing person. They zigzag in and out of the scent until they discover its source. According to Sullivan, the canine super sleuths can even locate bodies under water.

In one of their most bizarre cases, ARDA dogs found the remains of a murdered woman buried in a stone wall. Police authorities arrested a man who was driving a missing woman's car. Disgustingly, the suspect carried the woman's scalp with him, so the police were certain that he had murdered her and disposed of the body.

After a weeklong search in which they found various items that had belonged to the woman, the police remained without a corpse to prove that a murder had truly been committed. That was when they called ARDA.

Penny Sullivan recalled that their canny canines cracked the case almost immediately. One of the dogs pulled his trainer toward a rough stone wall near a cabin that the suspect had burglarized. Although it seemed impossible to suppose a stone wall could yield any productive clue to the missing woman, the dog stood firm and insistent.

ARDA's handlers stood behind their dog's keen senses, and the police authorities ordered the wall dismantled. The shocking truth was that the woman's body had been buried by her murderer within the stone wall.

ARDA is called in on about 100 difficult cases each year. The volunteer handlers even pay their own expenses to fight crime and to find missing persons.

Penny Sullivan insists that their reward lies in cracking tough cases.

• Chapter Sixteen •

How Animals Lead Scientists to Nature's Medicine Chest

Michael Huffman of Japan's Kyoto University and Mohamedi Seifu of the Mahale Mountains Wildlife Research Center, two primatologists conducting research in the jungles of Tanzania, had been observing a female chimpanzee who was so ill that she was unable to muster the strength to raise herself to defecate.

Suddenly the ailing chimp seemed to call upon a hidden reservoir of energy, and she managed to drag herself to a *Vernonia amygdalina* bush and began to suck loudly on its shoots.

The primatologists were astonished by the chimp's actions for two reasons:

1. Chimpanzees seldom touch the plant because it is so terribly bitter.
2. Native Tanzanians make extensive use of vernonia to fight parasites and gastrointestinal disorders.

By the next afternoon, the ill and enervated chimp's condition was very much improved. Her appetite had returned, and she was once again socializing with the other members of her community.

This was the first time that watching scientists had ever seen an animal's health improve after it had ingested a plant with known medicinal value.

And Huffman and Seifu believe that the chimp's reaching out for the vernonia was no coincidence. She seemed to seek out the specific plant in the same way that a human suffering from indigestion would reach for Alka-Seltzer in a bathroom medicine cabinet.

Michael Huffman also observed in two separate situations in the Mahale Mountains National Park, in Tanzania, that sick chimpanzes select this medicinal plant, which is hardly ever, quite possibly *never*, eaten by healthy chimps. The *Vernonia amygdalina* is used widely as a medicinal plant by people in many parts of Africa and has been proven exceptionally successful against parasites.

Since Huffman's and Seifu's discovery in 1987, researchers have now identified at least fifteen plant species that constitute what the scientists have come to term "the pharmacopeia of the apes." What is more, these same scientists have come completely to believe that the apes know exactly what they are doing. Evidence now abounds that primates discovered the curative potions, salves, and saps of nature long before their hairless human cousins.

Those researchers who have taken this astounding discovery seriously have found that the primates make use of potions from nature's medicine chest that effectively deal with everything from upset stomachs to cancers. Duke University primatologist Kenneth Glander has even reported a root that the howler monkeys use to practice birth control.

In March 1992, the American Association for the Advancement of Science devoted a session of its annual meeting to "zoopharmacognosy," the use of medicinal plants by animals. This first-ever symposium of its kind examined the questions of exactly how the practice evolved and whether or not primates and other animals can lead researchers to plants that may be medically useful to humans.

Numerous traditions among the various Native American, Native South American, and African tribes credit animals with providing medicine men and herbalists with valuable remedies and cures. According to Navajo legend, for example, it was the bear that taught the tribe that a species of the *Ligusticum* plant could treat a person bothered with a stomach ache, a bacterial infection, or a case of worms.

Harvard University ethnobotanist Shawn Sigstedt was aware that the shrub was still used by today's Navajo people for a variety of ills, but he wondered if it was truly a bear who had demonstrated the wonders of the ligusticum root to some long-forgotten medicine man. Deciding to put the old legend to a test, he conducted extensive research that convinced him that both captive and wild bears responded to the root like cats to catnip. Not only do bears in the wild eagerly seek out and dig up the root, but both the wilderness bears and captive bears will fight over the root.

When Harvard University anthropologist Richard Wrangham was with a group of fellow researchers tracking chimpanzees in Tanzania, he observed that the chimps would rise early in the morning to seek out *Aspilia* plants, a member of the sunflower family. It appeared that the chimps, extremely vulnerable to a host of parasites, seemed to understand that the plant contained a substance that helped their bodies get rid of the uninvited guests.

This appears to be a very deliberate and conscious act, as Michael Huffman had noticed in his own research that the chimpanzees with the worst cases of parasites ate the leaves which were the most bitter.

Biochemist Elroy Rodriguez of the University of California, Irvine, observed the same phenomenon of the chimps making a "beeline" for the aspilia plant. He remembered that they would swallow the leaves whole, then wrinkle up their noses and act like human children being forced to take a distasteful medicine.

Rodriguez identified the beneficial substance in aspilia as a red oil called thiarubrine, which is known to kill parasites, fungi, bacteria, and viruses. Additional laboratory tests inspired by the chimps of Tanzania produced evidence that the substance could also kill cancer cells of the sort that might be found in solid tumors such as those found in the lung and breast as well as—or even better than—commercial preparations.

The February 3, 1992, issue of *Newsweek* quoted Rodriguez as stating that this was the first time that "an animal has led us to a drug [whose structure and function] we have identified in detail."

Michael Huffman has noted that further underscoring the probably intelligent usage of medicines by the chimps is the discovery that the chimpanzees ate more of the aspilia and vernonia plants each year during the rainy season when they would be more susceptible to disease.

In other experiments it has been found that chimps *only* ate "medicine" when sick. Jane Goodall put tetracycline, an antibiotic, into bananas to feed to sick chimpanzees. She found that only the chimpanzees that were ill would accept and eat the laced bananas. Those chimps that were healthy would not eat the medicine-filled bananas. Once the sick chimps were healthy again, they stopped accepting the bananas.

It is still being researched as to how chimps "know" these things. It is interesting to note that since the first publications of the properties of aspilia, a range of observations has shown that elephants, bears, coatis, and capuchins all use natural chemicals as something other than food, according to the July/August 1994 issue of *The Sciences*.

Researchers Richard Wrangham of Harvard University, Michael Huffman of Kyoto University, Karen B. Strier of the University of Wisconsin, and Elroy Rodriguez of the University of California, Irvine all address the topic in a letter from readers in the Peer Review section of the magazine as stating:

"We can take such anecdotes and build them into evidence. In an era of shrinking biological resources, we don't think it's such a good idea to rely only on the studies of rats. Let's keep an open mind about ways of exploring the natural world. Who knows, out of little aspilia leaves big zoopharmacognosies might yet grow."

• Chapter Seventeen •

Two Different Points of View Regarding the Sovereignty of an Animal's Body and Brain

The use of animals in laboratory research provokes a discussion of scientific ethics and the rights of animals that becomes very complicated, extremely controversial, and usually very emotional, depending on the individual philosophies of those who debate such issues. Western science essentially maintains that humans have complete dominion over all animals and that a scientist may conduct certain worthwhile or necessary experiments on a laboratory animal without compunction.

At the same time, it is indicated in the Bible and in various ecclesiastical writings that animals are spiritually beneath humans and that they are devoid of souls and incapable of emotional responses. In other words, the Judeo-Christian religious traditions, as well as Muslim teachings, grant humankind dominion over their fellow creatures on planet Earth.

It is not within the designated parameters of this book to debate the matter of an animal's spiritual and physical sovereignty, but in the interest of expanding some readers' preconceived thoughts regarding the place of other species in the web of life, we feel it to be of value to examine briefly two cultures whose attitudes regarding the significance of animal life are quite different from the standard Western tradition of the total subservience of animals to human masters.

As we in the United States seek earnestly to understand better the Japanese people for purposes of economic and political harmony, we would make a giant step toward oneness if we could perceive that in their culture they make no sharp, hierarchical distinction between God, humans, and animals.

We hope that we may accept the promises of our own nation's research scientists when they swear that they treat their animal subjects as humanely as possible in experiments that sound horribly cruel and inhumane.

In Japanese research centers, however, it is common to find laboratory and field workers conducting memorial services and praying for the souls of those animals sacrificed in laboratory experiments.

According to an article in the March 2, 1991, issue of *New Scientist*, written by anthropologist Pamela Asquith from the University of Calgary, Japanese scientists include material in their domestic publications that they remove from reports submitted to journals in the United States and Europe. The excised material includes descriptions of "living things;" that is, subjective descriptions of the mental and personality traits of their animal research subjects.

Here on the North American continent, the native cultures believed in the unity and the cooperation of all forms of life. If it were necessary to take the life of an animal in order to survive, the creature was to be killed only after the hunter uttered a prayer, as if he were performing a sacrament. The individual soul of the slain animal and its group spirit had to be told that such an act of bloodshed was necessary for the turning of the great Wheel of Life.

The native people of North America had such respect for "the little brothers and sisters," "the four-leggeds, the winged ones, the water dwellers, and the belly crawlers" that a member of the animal kingdom stood as the surname of each traditional family. Ancient legends tell of the Great Mystery transforming certain members of the bear family, the deer family, the wolf family, and so on into two-legged humans, thus shaping the origins of the various tribal clans.

In the old days, individuals unhesitatingly traced their ancestral lineage from an animal, bird, or reptile. But whatever additional names the traditional people might acquire in their lifetimes, it was the totem animal identification that marked their soul and remained the name to which they answered when they went to the spirit world.

As our good friend, the late charismatic Chippewa medicine chief Sun Bear, once told us: "There is no need to argue about these things. If I say my ancestor was a bear and you say your ancestor was a chimpanzee, we don't have to fight over it, you know."

In *Warriors of the Rainbow*, William Willoya and Vinson Brown comment that men and women who follow the spiritual paths of the traditional native tribes are able to achieve a greater sense of harmony with all of life. The followers of the traditional medicine ways use "the animal spirit as a tool in reaching the Source of the World and in purifying the soul. . . . This was not idol worship . . . but something far deeper and more wonderful, the understanding of the Spirit of Being that manifests itself in all living things."

Too many of our better-educated men and women— those very people one would like to suppose might develop greater sensitivity to "all living things"—tend to place strict limits on the mental capacities of animals and are more likely to patronize, rather than respect, our "little brothers and sisters."

The early inhabitants of this continent saw themselves as relatives of the animal life around them. In the days of a traditional tribal existence, men and women participated in a very personal relationship with all animal life.

What a great tragedy it is that the great majority of contemporary men and women consider it necessary to widen the chasm between the natural world of Nature and animals and the artificial world of technology and civilization.

On the other hand, many of the traditional shamans and medicine priests of today believe that modern people can still develop the ability to blend with the consciousness of animals and once again enter the ancient realm of unity and oneness, and they are being joined in their assertion by a growing number of scientists who have begun to take a fresh, new look at animal intelligence.

Dr. Larry Dossey, former chief of staff of Medical City Dallas Hospital and a physician of internal medicine, suggests that to understand fully and to embrace the concept that we and the animals might be a part of a larger mind requires a genuine humility that allows us "to know deeply that consciousness is not the sole possession of an ego; that it is shared by not only other persons, but perhaps by other living things as well.

"It is humility that allows us to take seriously the possibility that we may be on a similar footing with all the rest of God's creatures."

Dr. Herbert Terrace, a psychologist at Columbia University, remarks that it has been difficult enough for the average layperson to admit that we humans are physically descended from, and related to, other species. After all, for thousands of years, human beings have believed that they alone, of all Earth's creatures, were capable of thought. And now, according to a great deal of new research, even our human minds are part of an evolutionary continuum.

• Chapter Eighteen •

Animals Who Make and Use Tools

A most interesting by-product of the many attempts to define more precisely animal intelligence is a reexamination of exactly what it is that constitutes human intelligence.

According to one orthodox view long nurtured by scientists, the human ability to make and use tools is what differentiates *Homo sapiens* from his primate ancestors and his contemporary chimpanzee cousins. But not many years ago, Jane Goodall's five-year sojourn among the chimpanzees in Tanzania's Gombe Stream Reserve prompted eminent anthropologist Dr. Louis S. B. Leakey to remark that "we must either redefine man, redefine tools, or accept chimpanzees as men."

Dr. Leakey's digs in Olduvai Gorge in Africa unearthed what many believe to be the world's most important and oldest anthropological site. Dr. Leakey is considered by most scholars to be one of the most prominent and productive anthropologists, if not the "father" of anthropology. Dr. Leakey and his wife, Mary, have dedicated their lives for nearly half a century to uncovering early man's remains in East Africa.

Jane Goodall, a determined and resourceful scientist, began her self-imposed exile among the chimpanzees in July 1960, with the encouragement of Dr. Leakey.

At that time, chimpanzees—the animals judged closest to humans, had never been studied for any prolonged period of time in their natural habitat. Goodall won the confidence of the potentially dangerous chimps and was able to gain from her relationship with them what anthropologists deemed to be *very* important results.

In her opinion, the fact that the chimps used twigs and grasses when feeding on termites was one of the most exciting discoveries that she made.

"It was known that some wild animals use natural objects as tools," Goodall said. "But the chimpanzee, when he strips leaves from the twig, is actually modifying a natural object to suit it to a specific purpose. . . . He is thus making a tool."

The chimpanzees were also observed crumpling leaves in order to fashion "drinking sponges." Goodall observed that the crumpling of the leaf increased the absorption and provided more water for the chimp.

She noted that chimpanzees are very fastidious in their natural habitat. Leaves are used to wipe sticky food off their hands and mud off their feet.

Her discovery that the chimps occasionally hunt and eat small monkeys was seen by some anthropologists as evidence to support the "natural killer theory," that is, that humans arose from carnivorous apes and that they first used chipped rocks and pointed sticks as weapons, not tools.

However, in an issue of *National Geographic* magazine, Goodall acknowledged the controversy in some scientific circles that turns on the question of whether early humans first used objects as tools or weapons, and she cautioned anyone from drawing concrete conclusions to support either side of the argument from her observations of the chimp community in Tanzania. "But the examples I have given amply demonstrate that these chimps, though seldom using weapons, have reached a high level of development in selecting and manipulating objects for use as tools."

Generally, Goodall said, the chimps work off their aggressions in energetic and noisy displays, rather than in actual combat.

According to prevailing contemporary theory, about thirty to thirty-three million years ago a creature like a gibbon, with long, swinging arms became the first step toward modern humans. This man-beast is known as *Propliopithecus*. Dental features peculiar to humans and the great apes appeared in *Proconsul* about twenty-five million years ago. These primates were followed by what has come to be considered the immediate predecessors of modern humans: *Australopithecus*, a hunter and toolmaker; and *Paranthropus*, a vegetarian.

Co-existing with *Paranthropus*, according to Dr. Leakey's theories, were *Homo habilis* and *Homo erectus*. In Leakey's view, these three species were constructing tools and hunting game over a million years ago. The most remarkable aspect of *Homo habilis*, the species the anthropologist considers the direct ancestor of modern man, was that he could rub his thumb and forefinger together and control that action with his brain. By contrast, Dr. Leakey has pointed out, the ape and chimpanzee can only grasp at something like a human with mittens on, with little control and with a great deal of arm movement.

But even with their "mittens on," as Jane Goodall observed, the chimps are using sticks, twigs, and leaves as tools designed to make their lives better and easier. And, of course, the chimpanzees are not alone among the animal species that demonstrate tool-making abilities.

For hundreds of years trappers and outdoorsmen have been in awe of the sense of community exhibited by the beaver. Naturalists have observed beavers plugging holes in their dams by gnawing off twigs and chunks of wood with such precision that they fit exactly the holes in need of repair. Such remarkable cooperation on the job indicates the ability to evaluate, measure, and somehow communicate to one another the areas of the dam demanding immediate attention.

When the lively sea otters find the tasty clams that they are seeking on the ocean bottom, they very often discover the annoying fact that dinner is firmly attached to a large rock. Undaunted, the otters solve the problem by gripping stones in their paws and hammering the clams loose. Certain otters have been observed carrying favorite "hammer stones" under their arms for ready use.

According to Dr. Donald Griffin, an associate of the Museum of Comparative Zoology at Harvard University, "There's a tremendous amount of evidence that demonstrates that animals work out problems and dilemmas just like people do. And because they frequently solve their problems with others of their species, it's obvious that they can 'talk' to each other."

In his book *Animal Minds*, Dr. Griffin recounts a case in which a dolphin memorized a complex manuever simply by observing another of its kind perform the feat.

"A female dolphin had learned to leap to a suspended ball, grasp it with her teeth, and then pull it through the water in order to raise an attached flag." When the female died, Dr. Griffin said, "A young male which had simply been watching the training sessions immediately stepped in and performed the entire trick. No additional training was necessary."

• Chapter Nineteen •

Animals with Unusual Abilities

Ruby the Painting Elephant

While Ruby may not have the biggest name in the contemporary art scene, she is certainly the biggest painter—for Ruby is an 8-foot-tall, 4.5-ton elephant.

Once a week, Ruby gives expression to her creative urges by painting a work of abstract art that may sell for as high as $1,200 and bring additional revenue to the Phoenix Zoo, where the seventeen-year-old Asian elephant resides. While a keeper holds a palette of paints for her selection, Ruby chooses the colors she wishes with a tap of her trunk, then accepts brushes dipped in the various hues to fashion her latest creation.

Now before you say that Ruby is just making haphazard swipes on canvas that her trainers and keepers laughingly refer to as actual paintings, be advised that the owner of an elegant Scottsdale, Arizona, art gallery says that the elephant has such a "distinctive and consistent style" that connoisseurs of abstract art immediately recognize her work.

For another thing, critics have long recognized that art is often born of frustration, especially when creative people feel that their need to express themselves is being blocked. Before Ruby picked up her first paint brush in 1987, she was regarded as a temperamental pachyderm that stomped ducks to death and swatted her keepers with her trunk.

Then one of her keepers, Tawny Carlson, noticed that Ruby seemed to like to make marks in the sand with her trunk, "as if she were doodling." Carlson was inspired to put an artist's brush in the elephant's trunk, set out some cardboard boxes, and—*voila!* Ruby began to paint. Today, there is often a four-month waiting list to purchase one of her master works, and she has brought in a great deal of money for the zoo's fund for endangered elephants.

Bill Gilbert, a wildlife writer, expressed his opinion that Ruby chose to paint for pleasure. Often, once a work is completed that seems especially to satisfy her, Ruby is seen to dance and to pat herself on the cheek.

Each original Ruby artwork is signed in the lower right corner with a distinctive squiggle made with a black magic marker.

Some of the other elephants in the Phoenix Zoo have appeared to become jealous of Ruby's paintings, so the keepers have permitted them to try their talent at a canvas. None, however, has been able to duplicate Ruby's unique style or her signature. Obviously, Ruby is a *big draw* for the zoo!

Sunset Sam

Sunset Sam, a dolphin who makes his home at the Clearwater Marine Science Center on Florida's west coast, is also a once-a-week painter who has made a name for himself among collectors of abstract art by creating works of strange and wonderful beauty. Sam beached himself in Old Tampa Bay in 1984, nearly died from pneumonia and intestinal parasites, and owes his life to the staff at the Clearwater center. He has repaid the debt many times over by earning thousands of dollars for his unique creations.

Even though he suffers from blindness in one eye, once a week, with the assistance of trainer Amy Baird, Sam selects his brush, then the colors, and begins to paint on canvas. It takes the porpoise Picasso two sessions to complete one painting, but it is easy to see that he enjoys each brush stroke.

Of course the dolphin needs help with the art supplies, so the trainer sets the brush, paints, and canvas on a specially made float that is accessible to the dolphin and stabilized in the water. If you have ever seen a dolphin show at a marine or sea park, or on television, then you have seen their uncanny ability to bob straight up and down as if walking or dancing on their tail fins. They seem to be able to do this for an almost unlimited amount of time; remember, dolphins are mammals and breathe air. So after Sam takes the brush in his mouth, he paints away!

Batir the Talking Elephant

We've all been impressed by the amazing circus tricks that the colossal and clumsy (in appearance anyway), elephants perform, despite their size, with grace and ease. They'll pivot on one foot while delicately balancing a whimsical damsel posed on their trunk, dance to the rhythmic beat of a lively song, and even scratch out a count on the circus tent floor, answering a question asked by their trainer, such as, "How many peanuts do you see here?" But have you ever heard of an elephant that talks?

As completely far-fetched as this might sound, in Karaganda, a city in Kazakhstan, (the former Soviet Union's second-largest republic, located in the south central part of the country, about 1,500 miles southeast of Moscow) reported in 1983 that they have an elephant that talks! The Karaganda Zoo claims that Batir, a baby elephant, *talks* . . . and that zoologists have tape recordings to prove it!

The then-official Soviet news agency gave the account to The Associated Press. Here is the full *Tass* account of the development:

> Once upon a time, the watchman at the Karaganda Zoo discovered that the baby elephant Batir, talks during the night. Naturally, no one believed the watchman's story: elephants are not on the list of animals capable of imitating human speech.
>
> Nevertheless, zoologists decided to check the truth of the watchman's claims. Armed with tape recorders, they went off for a night watch at the zoo. And they were rewarded. Batir spoke nearly 20 phrases into the tape recorders. His "interview" was even transmitted on local radio. The elephant speaks mainly about himself and his needs. "Batir is good. Batir is a fine fellow. Water. Have you watered the elephant?"
>
> The specialist explained this phenomenon by noting that the elephant was orphaned at a very early age. He was raised by humans from the time he was a baby. He learned some of the simplest phrases from his human parents. And besides all that, they say the elephant has exceptional hearing compared with other elephants.

The Associated Press called Karaganda to obtain a copy of the tape. Zoo director Nikolai I. Yepifanovsky said he would make a copy and mail it to the AP bureau in Moscow.

So, if it's true that elephants have an excellent memory, then be careful what you say to an elephant—he just might repeat it!

This Mailman Doesn't Worry about Dogs—He's a German Shepherd

The old comedy routine about the mailman and the vicious neighborhood dog has long ceased to be considered humorous by letter carriers around the globe, and today most postal delivery personnel carry Mace or some other canine deterrent along with the mail. In the tiny country town of Berne, France, however, Cosak, a husky three-year-old German shepherd, *is* the mailman, the only known canine letter carrier in the world.

Jean François Pichon, Cosak's owner, loads him up with as much as 30 pounds of mail in a backpack that he had specially made for the big dog. Cosak barks to let each resident know when the mail has arrived. If a house has a gate, he will jump up on it and ring the bell with his paw.

Although Pichon may be the "official" mail carrier for the 1,500 Berne residents, he insists that he feels as though he is Cosak's assistant. On those occasions when he may reach in the backpack to remove a special letter, Cosak still insists that he be the one who actually delivers the envelope to the resident.

Pichon said that he is completely confident that if for any reason he could not accompany Cosak on the route, the German shepherd would be fully capable of delivering the mail on his own.

Some years ago in the United States, a shepherd dog was the only mail carrier between the towns of Calico and Bismarck in California's Mojave Desert. According to local residents, during the three years of his assigned duties, Dorsey, the canine postman, never once missed his regular schedule on the three-mile route.

Francis the Superpig, a Canadian Folk Hero

Remember the University of Georgia research we mentioned earlier, which rated the pig as *smarter* than the dog? Well, here's a story of a pig who not only was smart . . . he wanted his independence!·

Francis began to carve a niche for himself among the great hog heroes of history one fateful day in 1960 when he seemed to sense that he was about to become a slab of bacon, and he made his escape from an Edmonton, Canada, butcher shop just days before he was scheduled for the chopping block.

In his desperate bid for freedom, the determined porker jumped a fence and walked quietly through a sausage-making room while the workers' backs were turned. He then managed to unlock a door with his snout, and made a mad dash for the nearby woods. (Even though it might sound impossible that a porker could jump a fence, it happens all the time. So much so, that most farmers have very high fences, some with barbed wire or electric shock wiring and the like to make sure the pigs don't escape.)

Later, as word spread of the proud pig's escape from the pork chop factory, local residents expressed the sentiment that Francis had won the right to life and to be left alone to enjoy his freedom.

Even the mayor of the nearby town, Red Deer, said that the noble hog embodied the Canadian spirit of freedom and bravery.

Francis, the pig with pluck, became a hero among swine lovers everywhere. He made a simple home for himself near some railway tracks and valiantly defended his porcine person by driving away hungry coyotes seeking to add pork to their diet.

• Chapter Twenty •

Animal Security Guards

Speaking of ancients, the Roman writer Pliny and many others observed that cranes have a very sophisticated guard system set up among their flock, which serves to protect them. There is always a crane designated for "guard duty" that is required to stand in the water on only *one* of those long spindly legs, while holding a stone in the other.

Imagine yourself standing on one leg and bending the other leg at the knee and holding in that same foot a stone between your toes. It certainly might look peculiar, to say nothing about how uncomfortable it would soon feel, but it does serve a very wise and intelligent safeguarding purpose.

If the required member of the crane flock who is on "active duty" should happen to fall asleep or even doze for a second, the stone will fall from its foot and awaken it with the splash of the stone hitting the water.

In fact, many animals seem to have a defense mechanism that warns family and community members of impending danger. Beavers slap the water with their flat paddle-like tails. Rabbits thump the ground with their hind legs; quail drum their wings, and so on.

The saiga antelope also appoint a guard from the herd to stand watch. The antelope on duty will not rest until the next antelope takes over. Researchers say that the antelope who is replacing the "guard" does so after giving a signal (much like a password). This password is supposed to ensure that the sentinel can't be tricked by another antelope that is not the "official" assigned guard.

It would be interesting to know the process of how the guard is assigned duty and by whom. Is it the whole flock that decides somehow, or do they make certain that all capable antelopes have an equal share in the responsibility? In the near future, further study might reveal the process.

Crows post sentinels to be alert to impending harm. They even go to the extent of having daily drills and have been observed to have a form of selective service, according to Ernest Thompson Seton in his book *Wild Animals I Have Known*.

These and other observances are not new, as some very excellent research on animal intelligence dates back to the late 1800s. However, our technological era has provided us with many more tools and sophisticated equipment to do research with, and these things alone have added volumes to an ever-increasing and expanding data bank on animal intelligence.

One piece of equipment that has made possible an enormous amount of new and expanding data is the *zoom lens* for video cameras. Prior to the zoom lens on either video or still cameras, researchers were in the precarious position of attempting to get as close as possible to the animals in studying their behavior within the confines of their natural habitats. They did this while doing their best to be as quiet and unseen as possible, so as not to frighten them or alter their normal habit patterns with the presence of humans and machines.

The very sight of a camera sometimes would spark curiosity in some animals, like the chimpanzee, for instance, yet anger others such as bears and other animals that might be likely to attack or charge. Obviously, the lives of researchers were often compromised because of this. Today, zoom lenses are constantly being improved on, allowing us to see great distances with clarity and safety. The telescopic lens also allows researchers to be able to observe animals for longer periods of time without the stress of remaining absolutely quiet and still.

• Chapter Twenty-One •

Of Seals, Sharks, and Fishing Boats

Daryl and Gary Graffenreid had been struggling to stay afloat for over three hours after their small fishing boat sank on a late spring afternoon in 1990. The two brothers were very aware that they could not last for too long in the churning waters off Channel Islands National Park on the Southern California coast.

And as if the rough sea was not deadly enough, the area was infested with sharks.

Although he had only a water-ski vest to help keep him afloat, Daryl, thirty, decided that he would set out to swim toward land so he might get help. The nearest piece of solid ground was several miles away, but Daryl knew that the situation was becoming increasingly desperate.

He had not been long on his solo mission when he found himself joined in his swim by a number of curious Pacific eared sea lions. To Daryl's perspective, which was bordering on panic, it seemed as if the sea lions sensed his need for help.

Later, he remembered in particular one baby sea lion that came within arm's length of him and who seemed almost to be probing his thoughts with its large inquisitive eyes. "Go get help!" he shouted at the diminutive sea lion.

When the little fellow immediately swam off, Daryl was hopeful that the sea lion had somehow actually understood him and was setting off to do his bidding.

In the next few minutes, as he struggled to make headway against the waves, Daryl saw that he now needed help even more than before. He was being circled by several large sharks. One of them, he chillingly estimated, was over 20 feet long.

The fisherman felt himself growing weaker by the moment. The waves seemed to be getting larger, and they kept pushing him under the surface, filling his mouth and lungs with seawater.

He was beginning to lose consciousness, and he thought such a state might be a merciful one—for the encircling sharks were coming closer and closer.

And then, as if by some magic of Father Neptune, ruler of the seas, Daryl saw that fifteen or twenty sea lions had suddenly formed a protective wall between him and the sharks. In answer to his cries for help, the seals had formed a living barrier between his struggling body and the sharks' ravenous jaws.

Although he was thankful for the aquatic mammals' comprehension of their human cousin's pleas for assistance—and he was awestruck by their remarkable courage—Daryl was dismayed that he kept going under. To make matters worse, the ski vest was becoming waterlogged and would probably soon be more of an anchor to pull him under than an aid to keep him afloat.

The fisherman began to think of his wife and two

young daughters and what would happen to them if he were to perish. He thought as well of his father, whose heart condition would likely prove fatal when he learned of the deaths of his two sons. Daryl knew that there was a strong possibility that his brother, Gary, was already gone, so he prayed to God with renewed earnestness, asking that he be spared for the sake of his family.

Within the next few minutes, his prayers were answered fully when a U.S. Coast Guard vessel pulled along side of him. And he felt even more blessed when he saw that his older brother had been already been rescued. In point of fact, it had been Gary who had pointed the coast guard in his direction.

Later, Daryl told everyone of his new respect for sea lions. "If it hadn't been for them," he said, "I'd have ended up as shark food."

A ranger from Channel Islands National Park commented that curious sea lions often approach swimmers and divers to inspect them at closer range, but he had never before heard of their forming a living barrier to protect a human from shark attack.

At about the same time, on the opposite coast of the United States, the crew of a fishing trawler off the coast of Massachusetts was able to return the favor of salvation to a doe-eyed baby seal that was being circled by dozens of blue sharks.

Receiving a flash of enlightenment that the *Cinmar II* was her only hope of escape from the vicious, jagged teeth of the sharks, the six-month-old female seal jumped on the fishing boat's net, swam up the ramp, and hopped on board.

Apparently exhausted by the ordeal of her escape, the little lady located a secure spot in the stern and fell asleep for twenty-four hours.

Robert Robles, skipper of the *Cinmar II*, said that

when she finally awakened from her extended siesta, she seemed completely at ease with the crew, accepting bits of fish from them and even permitting them to pet her.

The crew members were, in turn, so taken with her that they blocked the drains at the bow and fashioned a shallow pool for her comfort.

Robles named her Cinmar, after his trawler; and after she had spent a few days eating, swimming, and basking in the sun as if she were aboard the *Love Boat*, he attempted to return her to the sea.

Cinmar, however, appeared to have decided that life aboard a fishing boat was the life for her.

When Robles returned to port in Hampton, Virginia, he made the decision that Cinmar would be better served at the Virginia Institute of Marine Science in Gloucester than as a crew member aboard the *Cinmar II*.

While on land, the skipper told the local press the story of the seal's dramatic rescue from a group of sharks, and he was surprised to hear from Captain Les Brightman of the trawler *Andy P.* that Cinmar had also been a passenger on board his vessel.

Three days before she had sought refuge from the sharks aboard the *Cinmar II*, the human-loving seal had clambered into a net from the *Andy P.* and boarded the trawler. According to Skipper Brightman, she had scampered about as if she owned the vessel, permitted the crew to pet her, and exuded a joyful attitude.

After three days, however, she had begun to bark and waddle back and forth in a restless manner that seemed to indicate that her visit with the crew of the *Andy P.* had come to an end.

The crew helped her overboard, and she swam off—perhaps only a few hours before she was attacked by the sharks and sought refuge aboard the *Cinmar II*.

When Captain Brightman decided to pay a visit to the Virginia Institute of Marine Science to see if Cinmar might actually be the same seal who had visited his trawler, Jack Musick, head of the marine mammal program, said that the seal acted as if she knew the skipper the moment he walked up to her.

Brightman asked her how she was and if she remembered him; and according to Musick, Cinmar waddled up to him and seemed to talk back to him, making little grunting sounds. Then she took a mackerel out of his hand.

Musick commented that Cinmar had "the sweetest brown eyes" he had ever seen. "I'd love to know what she's saying," he said.

• Chapter Twenty-Two •

Insects and Worms Can Do More than Buzz, Bite, and Crawl

Some years ago, the noted conservationist Joseph Wood Krutch expressed his opinion concerning our human responsibility toward all species of animal life in the thoughtful assertion that "we owe kindness even to an insect."

Few people, however, would believe that insects might recognize human acts of kindness toward them or that they might have the intelligence to reciprocate.

In the mid-1960s, friends and members of Sam Rodgers' family were mystified by the strange behavior of his bees after the man passed away and was buried. So were the qualified bee experts of Shropshire, England.

Old Sam was the local postman, cobbler, and handyman in the small county of Myddle. Although he always kept busy with a multitude of jobs, interests, and pursuits, everyone knew that his great love was for his bees.

Each day Sam would go out to the hives and care for the industrious and buzzing members of his bee community, all the while talking tenderly to the insects as if they could understand every word and every gesture of his goodwill and affection.

Then, one day, the benevolent bee keeper did not come to the hives. Sam Rodgers had died.

His family, aware of the old rural customs of Myddle, were familiar with the belief that someone must tell the bees that their master had died, or the bees would leave the hives forever.

Two of the bee master's children walked reverently down the path to the hives and solemnly "told" the bees of the passing of their beloved master.

On the Sunday after Sam's burial, parishioners of the little church in Myddle called to the parson to come out and see what was happening.

The Reverend John Ayling later said that he witnessed "bees coming from the direction of Mr. Sam Rodgers' hives, which were a mile away."

According to the parson and other eyewitnesses, the bees formed an enormous line and headed straight for their master's grave.

Certain of the parishioners said that it would not be stretching the imagination to say that the great line of bees looked very much like a funeral procession. Once the bees had circled Old Sam's gravestone, they flew directly back to their hives.

"I just don't know logically how to explain the visitation of the bees to Old Sam's grave," Reverend Ayling said. "The only answer I can come up with is that the bees had come to pay their last respects and to say their good-byes to their old master."

Crickets That Give the Weather Report

Crickets have been used to tell the temperature with amazing accuracy! If there is no thermometer around (or even if there is and you just want to test the cricket's weather forecast), when you hear the chirp of a cricket, this is what you do to get the temperature outside. Listen very carefully and count the number of chirps the cricket makes in 14 seconds. Add the number 40 to that number. The total number of the two gives you the exact temperature in degrees Fahrenheit. This will work only if the temperature is 55 degrees or higher. Crickets will not sing on nights when the temperature is below 55 degrees. In fact, they like warm weather; the warmer the weather, the more actively a cricket will sing. They rest during the day and become active at night. (Don't we know . . . ever hear a cricket when you are trying to sleep?)

Maybe you will even wish to follow a centuries-old tradition from Japan. For hundreds of years, many Japanese have kept crickets as pets. They are called *suzumishi*, and thousands are distributed in tiny bamboo cages each summer to help people forget the heat.

Fiddle-Playing Crickets

Only male crickets have the tools necessary to make cricket music. They have their own built-in instrument, which is very much like a fiddle. Each of the male's wings has a rough surface on its underside called the file. In the same place on top of each wing is a scraper. Rubbing the scraper of either wing against the file of the other wing, the male cricket is able to make the music, or chirping sound, in a very similar fashion as one might play the violin or the fiddle. This is the male cricket's courting music; he uses his song to attract female crickets.

Musical Animal Orchestration

It is interesting to note that all animals use some part of their body to make various sounds that scientists are beginning to understand as communication with one another. As the crickets, some of the sounds can be linked with various natural phenomena such as temperature, and many of them are rhythmical with a repetitive, measured beat.

Prairie hens, mice, and rabbits beat their feet in sounds like drumming to communicate. The male deathwatch beetles make a rapid ticking sound by "percussion" of a protuberance on the abdomen, striking it against the ground. A sound that is very faint but sounds like ticking is made by a tiny little beetle, *Lepinotus inquilinus*.

Fish make sounds by blowing air, clicking their teeth, and drumming with select muscles against tuned air bladders.

The woodpecker and certain other bird species bang their heads in a type of drumming. The songs of most bird species have been analyzed extensively. Birds have a complex glossary of warning calls, alarms, and calls for recruitment, bringing help, or demanding dispersal for protection. They have mating calls, location calls, and just "songs."

Leeches have been heard tapping rhythmically on leaves to engage the attention of other leeches who tap back on leaves in synchrony. You've heard toads sing to each other on a warm summer's night, haven't you? One toad will sing out and his friends sing back to him in a chorus.

Alligators, crocodiles, and even snakes make various

sounds somewhat like vocal sounds; others who have loose skeletons rattle them. The rattlesnake, of course, rattles his rattler—one communication we all recognize and hope we never encounter!

Tarzan didn't beat on his chest for no reason. He learned it from the gorillas, who actually *do* communicate by beating on their chests for certain kinds of discourse. And last but not least, even the lowly earthworm makes sounds—very faint staccato sounds in repetitive clusters.

An Intelligent Worm?

Can a worm be educated? Yes! At the University of Michigan, scientists used the common flatworm, which one is likely to see in streams and ponds, in an interesting experiment.

The worms were taught to crawl through a series of very difficult mazes—a task the worms did quite well.

Worms have another amazing ability—to regenerate. When cut in half, the worms can grow new body parts. The heads will grow new tails and the tails will grow new heads. Both new parts (after a worm had been cut in half) demonstrated the remarkable ability to follow the same mazes that the original uncut worms did!

In another amazing experiment a trained worm was cut up into tiny pieces and fed to untrained worms that had been taken fresh out of the streams. The untrained but well-fed worms were placed in the same maze. Although the new worms had not been in the maze before, nor had they been trained in the maze, the worms that they had been fed had. The new worms mastered the maze—just as their "dinner" had done. They followed the maze correctly.

The scientists who conducted this experiment concluded that the memories of the worms that had been trained somehow had been integrated into the memories of the worms that ate them, allowing them to go through the maze!

Now, even though this sounds totally far-fetched, many such experiments have been done in order to find out *where* memory is stored, and to test various theories about the brain and memory.

Paul Pietsch, a biologist at Indiana University, was very opposed to theories and claims of other scientists that the brain appears to be holographic in nature, and that therefore memories would not possess any specific location in the brain.

Karl Pribram, a neurophysiologist at Stanford University and author of the classic neuropsychological textbook *Languages of the Brain*, along with a protégé of Einstein—David Bohm, a physicist of the University of London—are two of the architects and main proponents of the holographic brain theory. In order to prove them wrong, Pietsch devised a series of experiments.

In previous tests conducted by Pietsch, he discovered that even though he removed the entire brain of a salamander, it would remain alive but in a stupor state. Once the brain was replaced, the salamander would return to normal. Pietsch had even experimented with putting the brain back in the salamander in reversed, flip-flopped position, changing the location of the left and right hemispheres, yet nothing affected the salamander's behavior once the brain was back in—the salamander's normal patterns returned.

More and more confused as to how and why this was possible, Pietsch resorted to more drastic and extreme measures. He sliced, diced, flipped, shuffled, subtracted, and even minced the brains of salamanders in over 700 operations—always replacing the brain in its perilous condition back into the salamanders (what was left of their brains, that is!).

His extraordinary findings turned Pietsch into a believer of the "holographic" or "cellular brain" theory. His discoveries received national and international attention and were reported in a feature segment on the popular newsmagazine television show *60 Minutes*. Pietsch records his experiences in his provocative and insightful book *Shufflebrain*.

• Chapter Twenty-Three •

It Has to Be Love!

Little Lauren Transforms 2,000-pound Fierce Rhino into a Love Rag

Everyone knows that the rhinoceros is perhaps the most fierce and unpredictable of all creatures on the planet. What is more, quite honestly, it is probably one of the least attractive beasts imaginable, very much like a grotesque monster that managed to survive prehistoric times.

We have all seen those remarkable wildlife movies wherein the raging rhino charges the photographer's Jeep and nearly overturns it with its massive bulk and mammoth horn; and if we were to remember only one lesson from the film, it would be to avoid crossing a rhino at all costs.

What then should we make of the strange but wonderful relationship between a cute little blond eleven-year-old girl named Lauren and a giant beast of a black rhino named Momo, who is considered so fierce and unmanageable that even his keeper won't enter his pen?

John Booker, who owns the farm near Sandton, South Africa, where Momo has his home, said that he knew of no game ranger who would come near the 2,000-pound monster's pen without first firing a tranquilizer dart into him.

Yet little Lauren Gordon jumps into Momo's pen and even pets the brute's huge horn. As incredible as it seems, within minutes Lauren's very presence transforms one of Africa's most dangerous wild animals into a one-ton love rag.

Lauren first jumped into Momo's pen one day in 1992, and her father, Ron Gordon, said that he was terrified. He screamed at her to get out of the pen at once before the rhino charged her.

Lauren, however, simply smiled in beatific calm and told her father to relax. "It's okay, Daddy," she said.

And as astonishing as it seems, Ron Gordon remembered that somehow he believed his daughter. It appeared obvious from the first moment that Lauren stepped in Momo's pen that she established an instant line of communication with the behemoth that everyone said was incapable of being contacted by anyone or anything.

Momo even likes to be fed by Lauren, and he will eat directly from her hand. The girl talks to her giant friend as if he were a human, and some magic intonation in her voice causes Momo to respond to her with loving gentleness.

Momo's pen is still strictly off-limits to everyone else, though. He is strictly a one-woman rhino, and he has not given the slightest indication that his love for Lauren is transferable to anyone else.

Recently, a newspaper photographer who was assigned to take a few pictures of the little beauty and her massive beast was chased up a tree before he could aim his camera. A word or two from Lauren, however, and the photographer was permitted to climb back down and take the pictures he wished.

No one has ever seen anything quite like the friendship between Lauren and Momo. She is completely confident that Momo would never hurt her. "He loves me as much as I love him," she said.

A Mountain Lion Is Their Adopted "Daughter"

Pat and Steve Steinert of Fort Collins, Colorado, are two more unique individuals who have created a loving relationship with an "untamable" wild animal. A few years ago, the Steinerts adopted a mountain lion as their "daughter."

When they first acquired her in 1988, the sickly cub was skinny and malnourished; two years later she was a strapping 100 pounds and still growing.

When the scrawny female lion first came under their care, the Steinerts named her Alyssa and set about rebuilding her health. Alyssa had been confiscated from an owner who had purchased her illegally, and no zoo would accept her because she had developed osteoporosis, a condition that weakens the bones.

In the manner of two devoted parents with a human baby, the Steinerts took turns getting up in the night to provide Alyssa with bottle feedings. After a few months of tender loving care, the lioness was eating meat and devouring jars of baby food.

Each morning, Steve Steinert, a research biologist, takes her for a run with their two black Labradors. The once sickly cub soon works up an appetite for her regular diet of raw meat, three large cans of cat food, and about 40 pounds of chicken necks.

While Pat Steinert does not encourage just any family to acquire a mountain lion as a pet, she speaks lovingly of Alyssa. It must be pointed out, however, that Steve is a research biologist and Pat is a registered wildlife rehabilitator. Before she bonded so tightly with Alyssa, Pat had cared for deer, fox, wild rabbits, and ten other mountain lions.

Not just any family could adjust to a king-sized cat that purrs ten times louder than an ordinary house kitty. And not every family would want to face the food bills necessary to keep a full-grown mountain lion from getting the munchies and eying the neighborhood poodles.

Alligators Are Her "Babies" and She Feeds Them by Hand

If you would find it difficult to raise a mountain lion as your "daughter," then you would probably turn an immediate thumbs down on referring to 12-foot alligators as your "babies." Such, however, is not the case for Annie Miller of Houma, Louisiana.

Alligator Annie, as she is known to the locals and the tourists alike, has the gators eating out of her hand, and she calls her brood by their individual names. As the huge creatures cluster around her boat, she feeds Mike, Rocket, Fifi, and all the others out of her hand. Waiting until they are summoned for their respective turns at the goodies that "Mama" has brought them, they rise up out of the water to snatch chicken legs and thighs out of Annie's fingers.

According to Alligator Annie, the gators have learned to recognize the sound of her voice when she calls to them—and she can identify each of them by their individual characteristics.

Pushing eighty years of age, Annie was reared in the bayou country, and she learned as a very small child to respect the monster water dwellers with their massive, powerful jaws.

Although she dearly loves her babies and they nibble

tidbits out her hands as if they were house pets, Annie always treats them with caution. She never tries to pet them or to become too intimate with the scaly brutes.

Rats Incredible!

Cindy Carroll of Tabernacle, New Jersey, fell in love with rats when she was sixteen years old. A friend of hers had a pet rat that was very loving and very intelligent. Cindy was astonished when she saw that the rat would play "fetch" with a small ball, and it was obvious that the rodent was openly affectionate with her friend.

Today, Cindy Carroll and her husband, David, have nearly 200 of the scampering rodents in their home, and she insists that all of her bewhiskered friends have individual personalities. They all have sophisticated names, too, like Amadeus, Socrates, Cashmere Champagne, and Apricot Splendor. She stresses that there are no sinister Willards or Bens in the Carroll rat pack.

The furry critters dine on tuna fish, dog biscuits, sunflower seeds, Cheerios, and assorted vegetables. The Carrolls keep them in thirty large aquarium tanks in two of their four bedrooms. Mother rats can bear as many as fifteen babies per litter, so Cindy spends many nights assisting with natal deliveries and caring for the new arrivals. As the animals mature, however, they may be sold for as much as $50 each.

Although the rats are usually confined to their own two bedrooms, on occasion Cindy likes to bring certain of her favorites to join her in bed while she watches television with her husband.

David Carroll said that he had a difficult time at first getting used to married life in a houseful of rats, but he admitted that the rodents are now a part of the family. He does, however, confess to drawing the line when Cindy attempts to bring them to bed.

• Chapter Twenty-Four •

Watch Who You Call "Birdbrained"!

Birdbrain" gives birds a bad rap, insinuating that because their brains are so small in size, they must not have much gray matter for intelligence or learning. You've probably heard the expression applied to people as well.

In the past, the fact that some birds, especially household pets, like parakeets, parrots, macaws, and the like, can talk was attributed to mimicry. The copycat or parodied words were not necessarily a sign of intelligence.

All of that has changed in light of accumulating and continuing data from bird research scientists. This chapter should give you some insight into the reason many researchers are considering some birds as intelligent as chimpanzees—with abilities never even considered before.

New Research Labels Parrots "Flying Primates"

Certain species of birds are being put in the same category as dolphins and chimpanzees. Biologists who know parrots well use phrases such as "flying primates" and "honorary primates" to describe their intelligence and their complex social life.

Although parakeets, parrots, myna birds, macaws, and others have long been known to talk (sometimes repeating embarrassing words or phrases), it's always been thought that they were just good mimics and not capable of more complex tasks.

It would seem logical to wonder why this information is only now coming to light. With parrots, it would seem that their proficient mimicking ability alone would have prompted scientists to conduct more extensive research on their potential capabilities, discovering their intelligence long before now. In actuality, relatively few have been done.

According to an article in *The New York Times*, many scientists have not been eager to study parrots in the past because they are difficult to research in the wild. Their native tropical forests, which are usually very thick with foliage, cloak their activities. As laboratory subjects they are stubborn and cantankerous, not the most cooperative candidates to investigate.

New data reveals that parrots can deal with abstract concepts, communicate with people, understand questions, and make reasoned replies. This is amazing information. Saying that the parrot can deal with abstract concepts, listen carefully to questions, and give an answer that has been "thought out" changes entirely our whole concept of the animal kingdom.

Linking this with the new research coming out on dolphins, whales, and chimpanzees indicates that we may have to rethink our position of what separates the animals from humans.

The ability to rationalize and reason used to be one of the central and main differences that distinguished man from beast. Philosophically, it was even thought that the aptitude for reasoning meant the presence of a soul and was what separated higher from lower intelligence.

Alex, the Thinking Bird

One of the recent projects that has attracted much attention is that of Dr. Irene Pepperberg. Formerly of Northwestern University in Evanston, Illinois, Dr. Pepperberg spent more than twelve years studying the cognitive processes of one African gray parrot (scientific name, *Psittacus erithacus*).

Recently, as an ethologist at the University of Arizona, Dr. Pepperberg has been probing the limits of parrot mental ability. "Basically," she said, "we've shown that the parrot is working at the level of the chimpanzee and the dolphin." Dr. Pepperberg goes on to explain that Alex, the African gray parrot she has been studying, has demonstrated an understanding of abstract concepts at a level that in the past has been attributed only to primates and, more recently, dolphins.

Orphée the Magpie Rescued Her Canine Friend Kim

While most people assume that a bird is incapable of demonstrating any kind of concern or affection for any living thing other than its mate or its young, such cases as that of Kim the dog and Orphée the magpie indicate a much wider range of emotions for our feathered friends.

Orphée and Kim had been raised together as pets by the Roulet family of Vouziers, France; so when Kim disappeared one day in the fall of 1992, the magpie appeared to be as concerned as the other members of the family.

Everyone knew that it was not like their faithful dog to wander off, but they were faced with the sad reality that he was nowhere to be seen. They also had to face the remarkable situation of Orphée's broken heart. The magpie was so upset over his friend's disappearance that he did not eat for four days.

And then came the day when Orphée jumped off his perch, flew through an open window, and disappeared into the forest.

Now the Roulet family was doubly distressed, for it appeared that they had lost both of their beloved pets.

The next morning, however, Mr. Roulet was awakened by Orphée screeching at his bedroom window. Overjoyed that the magpie had returned, Roulet was puzzled when the bird continued its screeching din and refused to enter the house.

At last the pet owner became convinced that he should follow wherever the magpie wished to lead him.

"It was amazing," Roulet said. "Orphée lead me straight to Kim. The poor dog was near death. He had somehow got a hunter's snare around his throat. He had managed to drag himself until he was only two miles from home, but it is unlikely that he would have made it without Orphée finding him and bringing me to his side."

Roulet carried his beloved dog home, and the family carefully nursed him back to health. Kim survived, thanks to his feathered friend Orphée, and the magpie and the dog are once again contented companions.

Amazing stories such as the previous one might be considered coincidence if it were not for esteemed research such as that of Dr. Pepperberg and others.

In the first stages of her research, Dr. Pepperberg taught Alex the English labels for eighty familiar objects. Deliberately following similar experiments that had been done with chimpanzees, Pepperberg discovered that Alex could group like objects together. She found that Alex could categorize objects according to color, shape, or material and could identify how many objects were present in collections of up to six objects.

Displaying an uncanny ability to determine the concept of which items were the same and which items were different, Alex showed Dr. Pepperberg that he was able to discriminate between totally unfamiliar items on the basis of abstract categories. For example, Alex could recognize the relationship between a green pen and a blade of grass.

In a common test involving unfamiliar items, Alex might be shown two objects at the same time, such as a piece of white paper that has five corners and a pink woolen pompom. Alex would then be asked the questions, "What's the same?" and "What's different?" He would be expected to respond in terms of color, shape, or material.

Alex surprised scientists by responding, "None." This indicates that he has been able to recognize the *absence* of a similarity between two objects as well as perceive the existence of similarities.

Dr. Pepperberg published her research findings with Alex in 1990, in *The Journal of Comparative Psychology*. She stated that Alex, who was fifteen years old at the time of the publication, was able to identify the shape, color, or name of an object about 80 percent of the time. Another example was a test in which Alex was shown a purple model truck, a yellow key, a green piece of wood, a blue piece of rawhide, and orange piece of paper, a gray peg, and a red box. Alex was then asked, "What object is green?" Giving the correct answer, Alex responded, "Wood."

In another test, Alex was shown a football-shaped piece of wood, a key with a circular head, a triangular piece of felt, a square piece of rawhide, a five-sided piece of paper, a six-sided piece of modeling compound, and a toy truck. The experimenter then asked Alex, "Which object is five-cornered?" "Paper," Alex answered.

With forty-eight similar questions, Alex gave the correct answers 76 percent of the time. He was 100 percent right with questions involving shape. Dr. Pepperberg interpreted these statistics as significant evidence that Alex understands the questions as well as the abstract concept of category. She elaborated that Alex "thinks" about the information in order to come up with an answer.

Dr. Pepperberg said that Alex has displayed an ability that children find hard to achieve. "Alex is able to distinguish between the concepts of bigger and smaller, biggest and smallest and middle; all of these concepts are normally difficult, even for children," she said. "This is not just stimulus-response." Pointing out that in order to answer the questions correctly, Alex must first be able to understand the questions, and then think about the information in order to communicate with humans.

Pepperberg isolates Alex's abilities as being significantly ahead of other birds' skills. A pigeon, for example, may learn to peck a key to show that two sequentially presented colors are the same or different. But it rarely seems to be capable of transferring this ability to unfamiliar items. The doctor says that the pigeons' responses are likely to be the result of associations between specific objects rather than an understanding of color as a category.

Dr. Pepperberg sets no limits on what could be discovered with Alex. "Intellectually, I don't know where Alex is going." Emotionally, however, she regards him as equivalent to a two-and-a-half to three-year-old child. He spends eight hours a day in the company of humans. "He is very demanding, and very interactive," she says. "People don't realize how much attention parrots need."

In a 1990 issue of *New Scientist* magazine, an article entitled "Who's a Clever Parrot, Then?" by Annabelle

Birchall, other scientists comment on the intelligence of the parrot. Caroline Pond, a biologist at the Open University in Milton Keynes, England, agrees with Dr. Pepperberg's summary of the intellectual and emotional intelligence and emotional demands of parrots.

Caroline Pond has had her own African gray female parrot, as a pet, for more than sixteen years. Pond says: "She is remarkably apt. You can see her thinking as she looks for the right word. Other times she just babbles, particularly in a crisis. She is extremely good at soliciting and getting attention."

The same article quotes Dr. James Serpell of the department of veterinary medicine at the University of Cambridge and its Companion Animal Research Group as saying that a person should not consider getting a parrot to keep as a pet unless they are prepared to devote as much time interacting with them as they would with a human toddler. Dr. Serpell says, "It's a full-time job." "Also, this 'child' never grows up, yet may outlive its owner and may have to be written into his or her will so someone else will continue the care," he says. Dr. Serpell expressed his observation that without this kind of attention, parrots are capable of humanlike depression.

Dr. Serpell states that the birds will suffer without attention because they are highly social birds. He goes on to say that parrots will suffer less if they are kept in large aviaries with other members of their own species. "The bred-in-captivity factor may help a bit, but you cannot escape from the animals' own genetic predispositions," he says. Although a parrot is permanently attached to just one partner, they live together in large flocks and groups, says Serpell. He says that some 90 percent of a parrot's time in the wild is spent in preening partners and foraging for food. Deprived of these activities (or lots of attention), intense boredom sets in.

Dr. Serpell has studied the communication among a

flock of Lorine parrots (*Trichoglossus*) caught in the wild in Indonesia, Australia, and the Pacific. "Parrots are like primates, very clever and manipulative. They are the flying primates, if you like," Dr. Serpell concludes.

The book *Parrots: A Natural History*, (Facts on File, 1990) by Dr. John Sparks and Tony Soper presents a variety of parrot facts. Dr. Sparks is a zoologist who heads the natural history unit of the British Broadcasting Company (BBC). Tony Soper is a writer and filmmaker with the BBC. In the book, which many experts claim is a very accurate survey of facts and lore, many fascinating characteristics of parrots emerge:

• Of the many species of parrots, some of the most popular are cockatoos, cockatiels, parrotlets and parakeets, lorys and lorikeets, amazons and macaws, caiques and conures, keas and kakapos, lovebirds, budgerigars, and just plain parrots.

• Many species live about as long as humans. A middle-aged person buying a young parrot as a pet is unlikely to outlive it.

• Most parrots mate for life, although divorce is common in some parrot societies. Mates go everywhere together. Unlike other birds, which avoid physical contact except in coition, parrots spend much of their time snuggling up to one another and preening each other.

• Parrot parents invest a lot of time raising their offspring. Like monkeys and apes, young parrots undergo training in family groups, where the wisdom of the elders is transmitted.

• Like primates, parrots play, some scientists believe. "Why else does a New Zealand variety of parrot called the kea, slide down the roofs of alpine huts on its back?" ask Dr. Sparks and Mr. Soper.

- A parrot's foot has opposable toes, two each in front and back, and is the closest birds come to having a hand. With this foot, a parrot can hang on to a branch and eat a seed or nut the way humans eat a sandwich.

- The budgerigar, a native bird of Australia, is the most widespread household parrot in the United States, where it is familiarly called a parakeet. Along with the abundant cockatiel, it would be exempted from a proposed legislation on bird imports.

- In captivity, the birds' mimicry flowers naturally. Dr. Sparks and Mr. Soper say, "No formal lessons are required." They give as an example Sparkie, a British budgerigar who got himself into the *Guinness Book of World Records* in the 1950s with a virtuoso performance in which he recited eight four-line nursery rhymes without drawing a breath!

Be Careful What You Say around an African Gray!

Pat Myers, a widow with two married children, had been happily running a chain of dress shops until she was stricken with an ailment that affected her vision and stamina. Confined to her house for a year while she was undergoing treatment, Pat felt as if she would go crazy with boredom and loneliness.

When her daughter Annie suggested a pet, Pat's response was that she didn't have the energy to walk a dog, she was allergic to cats, and fish just didn't have a whole lot to say.

Annie told her that birds had a lot to say. "Why not get a parrot?"

In the May 1991 issue of *Reader's Digest*, Jo Coudert

told the amusing and heartwarming story of Pat Myers' interaction with an African gray parrot that she named Casey.

Several weeks later, when Annie asked her mom how she liked her new companion, Pat replied just fine, but she never realized that Casey would pick up all kinds of words that she said.

The first sentence Casey had learned was "Where's my glasses?" That query was soon followed by "Where's my purse?"

Whenever Pat came back into the house after she had been out, Casey would greet her with, "Holy Smokes, it's cold out there!" in perfect imitation of her voice. Needless to say, Pat warmed up to the fact that she had a new housemate.

"It makes the whole house better just to have him," she told Annie one day. "I laugh four or five times every day—and medically laughter is supposed to be good for a person."

Casey was quite mischievous, however. Though he was allowed to roam free most of the time he occasionally had to be put in his cage, which he did not much care for. One time, when Casey was in his cage, a plumber came to call to repair a leak under the kitchen sink. Casey's cage was always kept in the den. The plumber who was working in the kitchen had no idea that Casey sat on his perch watching him through the open door between the kitchen and the den.

Suddenly, Casey called out, "One potato, two potato, three potato, four. . . ."

"What?" the plumber asked.

"Don't poop on the rug," Casey instructed, only in Pat's voice.

Insulted, the plumber marched into the living room where Pat was sitting and said, "What did you say to me?"

"I didn't say anything to you," Pat replied.

"Look lady," the plumber said, "if you're going to play games with me, you can get yourself another plumber."

Pat looked at him blankly, indicating that she had no idea what he was talking about.

Reluctantly and somewhat bewildered, the plumber asked, "That was you, wasn't it?"

Pat smiled. "Was what me?"

"The 'One potato, two potato ... poop on the rug' stuff," he said, sheepishly.

"Oh dear," Pat said embarrassed, but finally understanding what had happened. "I think I had better introduce you to Casey."

"What's going on around here?" Casey demanded as he saw Pat approaching his cage with the plumber in tow.

As they approached the cage, Pat sneezed and Casey immediately mimicked the sneeze, and also added a couple of coughs like Pat would do when her allergies were acting up.

The plumber, surprised, looked at Casey, and then at Pat, and back at Casey. He shook his head. "I guess I'd better go back to the sink," he said and laughed.

A few days later, while Pat was reading the newspaper, the telephone rang. She picked it up, but all she heard was a dial tone. "Hang-up," she said to herself. The next day it happened again. The phone rang, but when she picked it up there was only the dial tone.

By the third morning when she answered the phone and got only a dial tone, Pat finally realized that Casey had learned to mimic the ring of the phone so flawlessly that he had fooled her into thinking it really *was* the telephone!

Pat grew to respect more and more Casey's keen awareness. At times he seemed almost human, yet he did not hesitate to say things that a polite human wouldn't dare to utter.

She recounted a time when a visiting guest seemed to have forgotten to go home. They were standing in the doorway as the guest just went on and on, not seeming to know when to leave. From the other room, Casey yelled out impatiently, "Night, night."

Casey easily picked up all kinds of words, phrases, and responses without being taught. And in addition to the telephone he could mimic all kinds of sounds to perfection. He could mock the sound of dripping water, the doorbell, and many acoustic effects he picked up from television. No matter how many times Pat heard Casey duplicate these different sounds, they would often catch her off-guard. However, she couldn't get mad at such a talent—she would just get a good laugh out of the fact that she'd been tricked again.

Because Casey learned so much without being taught, Pat found it extremely exasperating that the one thing that she really tried to teach Casey seemed to go right by him.

She would sit in her comfortable living room chair, reach up and pet Casey's head and lightly stroke his velvety gray feathers and scarlet tail. "Can you say, 'I love you, Pat Myers?' " she would ask over and over again.

Casey would cock his head, look at Pat, and reply that he lived on Mallard View.

"I know where you live, funny bird," she would sigh in exasperation. "Tell me you love me."

To which Casey would simply respond with, "Funny bird."

Pat's health had improved to such an extent that she decided to go on a three-week vacation. Knowing she'd miss Casey but that she couldn't take him with her she left him with Annie and the kids.

On the day Pat was to return, Annie brought Casey home so he would be in the house to greet Pat when she walked in the door.

Casey appeared to be fine, but he just glared at her, moving as far to the back of the cage as possible.

Pat begged him not to be angry with her, but Casey dropped to the very bottom of the cage and huddled there, ignoring her.

She left him to his pouting, but in the morning she tried to warm up to him. Casey still refused to speak.

Later that day, Casey took a few uncertain steps up Pat's wrist. She pleaded with her pet, admitting that she had been wrong to leave him for so long.

"Please," she asked, "I know I've been gone for a long time, but you have to forgive me, Casey."

Casey took a few cautious steps up her arm, and then hopped on Pat's knee. Sensing his feelings, Pat looked at Casey and said, "Were you afraid I was never going to come back? I would never do that," she said understandingly.

Casey tilted his head, looking at his mistress carefully, then he slowly hopped up her arm. Pat bent her elbow as Casey finally moved closer and nestled up to her. Stroking his little head and smoothing his feathers gently with her forefinger, Pat was relieved when Casey finally spoke.

"I love you, Pat Myers," he said.

Wise as an Owl?

In a book about animal intelligence we must address the "wise old owl." People in ancient times used the owl as a symbol of wisdom. Maybe its large, bright, wide-awake look and the straight-on stare of the owl make it appear sharp or astute.

Actually, an owl does not have the ability to move its

eyes from side to side in the eye sockets. Its eyes point forward, where they can change their focus very quickly from near to far objects. Somewhat like a tele-photo lens, the owl's eyes can focus on individual objects instantly. This is a benefit in hunting for food. Even though the eyes cannot move, the owl's head can turn around completely to look behind it without moving any other part of its body. Perhaps this ability also added to the ancients' misconception that the owl is an intelligent or wise creature.

Actually, the owl is not a wise animal. For its size, the owl's brain is quite small. Geese, crows, and ravens are in fact smarter than the owl!

The Bird That Can Always Find Its Way Home

The homing pigeon has been known to travel more than 1,500 miles or more from its home over unfamiliar territory, and yet it will always return to its home loft.

• Pigeon School

Although the pigeon has a natural built-in instinct for getting back home, special training is often given to those used for message delivering. Its keepers release the pigeon for a short distance from its home and the pigeon quickly flies back. Gradually, that distance is increased as the pigeon grows.

• Special Delivery

Messages are placed in small metal containers attached to the pigeon's foot, and unless the pigeon is shot down, that message always gets to the intended delivery place.

The carrier pigeon has been known to be a reliable "delivery boy" for so long that even thousands of years ago, man bred pigeons for racing and for carrying messages.

Where did birds get their feathers? Billions of years ago, birds were once part of the reptile family and had scales that evolved into feathers. The feathers help keep birds warm by insulating their bodies. Feathers also are like having a built-in raincoat, as they keep the body of the bird dry. In addition to these smart adaptations, the feathers also enable the bird to fly—a flying serpent?

The feathers are appropriately fitted to each bird species according to its needs. For instance, the feathers of an owl are very soft and long, enabling it to fly quietly but slowly. The hawk's feathers are shorter, so it can fly more rapidly. Birds who live near or on water have oil covering their feathers, making them extra waterproof (thus the expression "rolls off like water off a duck's back").

An Annual New Suit of Clothes

All the feathers fall out, a few at a time. Once a year all the feathers of a bird will have been replaced in a process called molting.

The number of feathers each bird has varies greatly according to the bird. The hummingbird has the fewest—around 940. The whistling swan has the most—around 25,216. (That's a lot of feathers!)

The "Master Carpenter," Builder of Homes

The pileated woodpecker, the largest woodpecker in North America, exemplifies the essence of the Spanish word for woodpeckers, *carpinteros*, for the industrious bird serves as a master carpenter who provides homes for several other species.

Inhabiting both conifer and hardwood forests in each

Canadian province, as well as certain sections of the United States, the pileated woodpecker vacates his nest cavity each year to fashion a new one; and scores of wood rats, squirrels, and a wide variety of winged tenants compete to assume instant ownership of the old "apartments."

It is no easy matter hammering out a home in a sturdy tree trunk with only one's beak to use as a tool, but the pileated woodpecker manages to excavate a nest cavity that averages about 22 inches deep and 8 inches wide. For security purposes and to protect the young from predators, the nests are about 40 feet off the ground.

In the February 1993 issue of *Wildbird*, Dr. Evelyn Bull, a research wildlife biologist for the U.S. Forest Service, writes that if it were not for the efforts of the "master carpenter" pileated woodpecker, such species as saw-whet owls, bluebirds, chickadees, Northern flickers, bats, tree squirrels, flying squirrels, and bushytailed woodrats would have far fewer nesting and roosting cavities.

The male hornbill protects its mate and their eggs by finding a hiding place for them in a hollow tree. Once the female has been made comfortable, the male methodically gathers mud and plasters over the only entrance to the hideaway, thus sealing his family behind an adobe wall. Only a small slit is left in the wall to allow the male to pass food to his mate.

The stilt, a long-legged bird of New Zealand, has learned to emit a cry that mimics the yapping of a dog, thus frightening away predators.

One of the most intelligent birds in the world is said to be New Zealand's kea, a chicken-sized green parrot that lives for most of the year above the snow line in that island nation's Southern Alps. Although New Zealand officially put the bird under partial protection in

1954, its numbers have been severely reduced because of the state of siege between the aggressive kea and the farmers who attempt to protect their crops against its periodic plundering.

Motorists driving through Arthur's Pass Park may find their windshield wiper blades carried away by the remarkably bold and curious kea. Roadwork crews arriving in the morning may discover their tractor cushions ripped to shreds and all the wires torn away from the motors.

Such activities are humorous and mildly annoying to some, not at all funny and costly to others. And certain farmers have been claiming since settlement days in the 1800s that the kea has developed a taste for mutton and kills sheep in a wanton manner.

Worth Matthewson, an Oregon-based writer, sacrificed a number of automobile accessories to the kea while photographing the intelligent parrot; but he learned that most New Zealanders appear to have a tolerant affection for the cheeky birds.

Trumpeters, large South American birds, are trained in Brazil to stand guard over other more vulnerable and defenseless poultry.

The cautious firetail finch of Australia approaches his nest, then pauses, and utters a "password" call at its entrance. He will not enter the nest until his mate sounds the counter call that assures him it is safe for him to join her.

• Chapter Twenty-Five •

Dolphins and Whales, Submerged Mammals Whose Intelligence Emerges

Nearly three-quarters of our planet's surface is covered with water. From space, astronauts have said the earth looks like a great big blue marble. Perhaps it is with this view that we can truly comprehend what mysteries might be hidden in the depths of the seas. Some of the most marvelous of these mysteries are the mammals of the sea: dolphins and whales.

The Whale That Worked for the Whalers

"Old Tom" was a most unusual killer whale that killed for man. So said the whalemen, at least, who lived in a little town called Eden, in New South Wales. They told a captivating story of an unusual working relationship between man and whale.

For many years, in the early 1900s, every winter Old Tom seemed to have a sense of when the whalemen would be setting out to hunt whales. Old Tom would be waiting offshore along with his whale companions, eager and ready to assist the fishermen in their hunt.

As soon as the whalers spotted Old Tom, they would jump in their boats and row out to the whales—not to kill them but to take them up on their willingness to corral other whales.

An extremely rewarding alliance, the killer whale pack would lead the whalers to a gigantic quarry of another species of whale, usually humpback or fin whales, and drive the catch into shallow water where the whalers could easily take over.

The killer whales worked with incredible skill. While the fishing boats sat patiently nearby, two killer whales would seize a victim's tail to stop it from thrashing and flailing about while two more whales swam beneath its head to prevent its escape by diving. Then the remainder of the pack would close in on the cornered, hunted whale.

As if all this weren't enough, one by one the killer whales would take turns hurling themselves out of the water and onto the captured whale's sensitive blowhole. They would continue to do this until it was so stunned and breathless that it rolled over and slipped beneath the shallow waves, and the whalemen would then plunge their lances into the helpless whale.

As the hunted whale was dying the killer whales would fight over their reward—the tongue and the lips of the victim—then they would head back out to sea. The whalemen usually waited for a few days until the carcass of the dead whale rose to the surface to tow in the rest of the whale.

No one seems to know just how or why this unusual hunting pact developed between man and whale. Old Tom demonstrated an uncanny understanding of the methods that the whalers used. Even when there were no boats at sea ready for a hunt, at times Old Tom would have the pack of killer whales surround a whale, then detach two or three of their own group in order to alert the whalers.

The whales would actually use their flukes to slap the water offshore until the fishermen heard them and put their boats out to follow them to their prey.

Strangely, when Old Tom died, (the whalers found his carcass on a beach in New South Wales), the whaling pact ended. Without Old Tom to lead them, the rest of the whales no longer awaited the company of their fishermen friends. Apparently the commitment to help the fishermen wasn't shared by the other whales without Old Tom's leadership.

Even though more sophisticated whaling techniques soon replaced the old rowing boats and the hand-held harpoons, the industry gradually died out in the town. But the town of Eden did not forget Old Tom. To this day the townspeople honor the memory of Old Tom and his allegiance to the whalers. Old Tom's skeleton is one of the Eden Museum's proudest exhibits.

Why Kill a Whale?

Organized whale hunting has been a way of life for many fishermen for over 200 years. Until the development of refined mineral oils, whale oil was one of the best and purest sources of lubricant known to man. For that reason, the sperm whale was in great demand. The giant, squared-off forehead of the sperm whale contains as much as 500 gallons of oil. The sperm whale was named by early hunters who erroneously thought the oil was the animal's sperm.

The Prized Product of a Whale's Indigestion

It is hard to imagine the human logic that would set a price tag of $100,000 on whale regurgitation, but that is just what a thousand pounds of whale "upchuck" sold for in London in 1912. Think of the value with today's inflation! The foul-smelling black matter is thought to be a result of intestinal irritation from the hard breaks of the thousands of squids that sperm whales swallow whole.

Most often ambergris, as the matter is called, is found floating on the sea in small lumps of only several ounces. With exposure to sun and air it develops a pleasant fragrance and becomes pale, turning nearly amber in color. Curious as it sounds, ambergris is extremely valuable to the perfume industry for its ability to hold a scent. Mixing ambergris with other perfume ingredients makes the fragrance last much longer, hence it has become a marketable commodity.

The whale is the world's largest animal, yet it feeds on some of the sea's smallest creatures. Baleen whales have hundreds of small plates, instead of teeth, hanging from their upper jaw. This type of whale gets its name from these plates, baleen. The baleen plates are made of an extremely flexible material, somewhat like our fingernails. These act like a filter to strain out the tiny food particles in the sea that the whale swallows as he swims with his mouth open, getting masses of plankton at a time.

The whale, a warm-blooded mammal, must breathe oxygen from the air in order to live; yet some can stay underwater for as long as forty minutes without coming up for air. When the whale surfaces, it takes in oxygen through the blowhole (like our nose). After filling its large elastic lungs, which are connected to the blowhole, with air, it then dives to feed in the ocean.

The air the whale has taken in heats up its body while it is underwater. When the whale surfaces, it exhales this air, much as we exhale after taking a big breath. What comes out the whale blowhole is called blowing or spouting. When the warm air from the whale meets the cool outside air, it condenses and turns to a steamy spray. This too could be compared to seeing our own breath on a cold day, but a whale's spout can shoot as high as 20 feet into the air and be seen from a mile away.

Killer Whales

Anyone who has seen the magnificent killer whales perform at a marine park will ponder how and why this whale obtained its name. Recent studies of whales reveal them to be amazing creatures with an intelligence, along with that of the dolphins, that we are just beginning to appreciate.

In the marine park amphitheater shows, the bond between the trainers and the whales is evident. Affectionate creatures, the whales get hugs, like to be stroked and rubbed, and playfully frolic. Responding to the learned commands of their trainers, they seem eager to please.

The level of trust is high—surprising even—as a whale that weighs many thousands of pounds (up to 6 *tons*) does a sort of water ballet with its trainer, culminating in a nose-push dive from the giant killer whale, thrusting the trainer some 20 feet into the air. This precision is a life-or-death matter, as too great a thrust, or one in the wrong direction, would be dangerous or even lethal to the trainer.

How the killer whales are able to move with such incredible speed through the water and then burst into the air with amazing grace to a height of 20 to 30 feet or more, pulling all their weight in complete precision and elegance, seems astounding! All this grace and playfulness is wonderful and mysterious to behold, but to be respected. Although there aren't many stories of killer whales attacking humans, they do kill.

The April 1979 issue of *National Geographic* magazine reported an incident of killer whales caught on film, somewhat by accident, which may in fact substantiate that their name is justly deserved after all.

The research vessel *Sea World* was about its business tagging swordfish for a migration study off the tip of the Baja peninsula in California. Milton C. Shedd, the owner of the boat and the chairman of the board of Hubbs–Sea World Research Institute, San Diego, spotted a patch of frenzied thrashing and whitecaps. Suspecting killer whales, Shedd alerted the helicopter that was aiding in the swordfish study.

From the air, the pilot confirmed that it was truly a pack of killer whales, caught in a rarely seen and never before photographed surprise act. A group of killer whales was attacking one of the most massive creatures of the sea—a young 60-foot blue whale. About thirty killer whales were relentlessly stripping away the flesh and blubber of the cornered blue whale.

The surprising thing to the scientists and researchers was the deliberate and intentional way the killer whales went after their victim. Just as in the story of the killer whale Old Tom (except in that case the whales cooperated with man in corralling other whales for the whale hunters), the whales seemed to have mapped out a plan of how to go about the kill.

It appeared that the whole attack had been intelligently masterminded. Acting in harmony, some of the killer whales would flank the victim on either side, as if herding it, while two other whales went on ahead and two stayed behind in order to foil any attempted escape. One group of whales seemed intent on keeping the blue whale underwater in order to hinder its breathing, while another killer whale swam under the blue's belly to make sure it didn't dive out of reach. The flukes had been shredded and the dorsal fin was chewed off by the time the researchers spotted the attack—another seemingly calculated effort.

The *Sea World* vessel followed the attack, which lasted until early evening and covered about 20 miles. How long the struggle had been going on before they discovered it is not known, but it went on for five hours after they came upon it. They reported that the attack mysteriously ended abruptly at about 6 P.M., and all the killer whales swam away. Amazingly, the blue whale, still alive, swam slowly on.

Although probably mortally wounded, why the blue whale was attacked in the first place, and why the killer whales ceased attacking their victim before the blue was dead are not known.

Not all whales have teeth. We have discussed whales without teeth, the baleen whales. Toothed whales eat fish, squid, and other sea animals. They use their teeth to capture their prey, not to chew them, because they swallow their food whole. This fact adds to the enigma of the killer whales' taking chunks out of the blue whale—torturing it—when it normally eats from a wide variety and takes its food by swallowing the delectable seafood whole.

Because the killer whales are so playful and smart when trained in captivity, many people think the whales are unfairly named, and many attest that killer whales would never intentionally hurt a human, much less kill one. Some even go so far as to say that a killer whale has never killed or harmed anything. Perhaps capturing this attack on film gave more than fair warning that we should have a healthy respect for the world of the whale. Trust is wonderful, but caution would be wiser!

This only points out with greater clarity the perplexity of studying any intelligent mammal. We would think it shocking, at first thought, that a whale could gang up on and kill one of its own, even though a different breed, for apparently no reason.

To be fair, instead of dismissing their intelligence after learning about such stories, if the situation were reversed and one of the whale species were observing us, they would likely be puzzled by our inconsistent behavior as well. They might encounter humans—generally playful, creative, inventive, and responsible—in a "drive-by shooting" or any one of thousands of murderous acts, to say nothing of *wars*. One certain truth is that no matter what the species, *intelligence does not always mean peaceful, harmonious, and fair!*

There has long been speculation and debate over the possibility that either dolphins or whales could actually be more intelligent than humans—if we could only learn to interrelate with them. The basis of this projected potential was usually fueled by their greater brain capacity. Some scientists now surmise that intelligence has less to do with the size of the brain than the ability of a sentient species to sustain itself harmoniously for a reasonable period of time.

Both dolphins and whales (cetaceans) have been on Earth for at least thirty million years. That is a very long time, in which they have had approximately the same form and yet have not destroyed themselves into near extinction; nor have they harmed the ocean in which they live. We humans have the dubious honor of being guilty of polluting the ocean waters in which they live ... as well as the air that both they and we breathe. Who would the cetaceans consider the sentient ones?

In fact, we are learning how very sensitive these giant whales might truly be. Perhaps there is some built-in sense that offsets ecological imbalance. Maybe something was wrong with the blue whale that had been attacked by the killer whales—a disease or illness. This seems to be nature's way and is seen throughout the animal kingdom. Questions like these and many others don't necessarily have definitive answers; yet the more we study them in their natural habitat, knowledge and understanding of their ways will likely increase.

Some of what scientists have recently learned has given us an appreciation for what in fact turns out to be a very delicate balance within the whale species. Their birthing process is still somewhat a mystery. Some of the whales (particularly the belugas) have a high rate of infant mortality. Even in the wild, some 50 percent of the beluga whale firstborn die.

Scientists have been studying the whale birthing process in order to understand just what happens that gives them such seemingly uneven odds at life's beginning. One of the Sea Parks captured one of the first whale births in captivity on film.

In analyzing the film, it was noted that the expectant mother whale spends many hours writhing and twisting, sometimes even thrashing about, in her attempts to wriggle her baby out. This extreme twisting might be too severe at times, and the mother may unintentionally do something that injures her young one.

We know that the mother whale is predisposed to motherhood and has more than an affectionate attitude toward her newborn. Whales have been observed to carry their newborn balanced on their forehead if it is born dead or if it dies soon after birth. The mama whale will continue to do this until the baby whale disintegrates, which can be many weeks or more.

In the wild, if a whale cannot hang on to her dead newborn in this manner, it will find a substitute like a plank or driftwood—even another dead carcass of something in the sea—as her surrogate calf.

In captivity, if the dead baby is taken away from its mother, the mother whale will even dislodge a buoy or carry a ball balanced on her head—anything she can find—always being careful to keep whatever is poised on her head exposed to the air, as if it needs to breathe. This ritual of grief and mourning is much like that of the apes (as described earlier, in the chapter on animal grief).

Whales Are Teaching Us a New Technology

Whale skin is 20 times more sensitive than a human's skin. Like dolphins, they use echolocation to communicate and to "see." Echolocation is the ability to perceive size, location, distance, density, and other aspects of objects by emitting sounds and analyzing their echoes. This echolocation is three-dimensional, enabling cetaceans to "see" *into* one another.

They can determine the health of all the body parts, because they can see all the internal organs and all the body's systems with this process. We are now using a more limited technology of ultrasound or echolocation as a form of X ray in hospitals in order to determine the health of human internal organs.

A sonogram uses much lower radiation than an X ray, yet gives just as clear a picture of the internal organs or anatomy in question. This lower radiation, of course, makes the sonogram safer; yet another advantage offers a more accurate "picture" of what is going on. For instance, if a doctor is trying to isolate what is causing a particular erratic heart rhythm in a patient, an X ray would show only what is occurring at the precise second the X ray is taken. With a sonogram, a continuous picture can be viewed as long as desired. We have witnessed our hearts under a sonogram; you actually *watch* your heart beating away in your chest—there it is on a television-like screen in front of you. An irregular heart beat then can be observed from moment to moment until a pattern may be determined.

Echolocation has also been used for many years by the navy, as well as to map the ocean floor for maps or exploration, and radar is used to locate planes and traffic.

There are *chemical* changes that occur in our bodies with all the varied emotional states. Scientists have been "mapping" these subtle changes that affect us so much they eventually lead to health or disease in our bodies, minds, and spirits. Dolphins and whales have the advantage that they don't need all the expensive technological breakthroughs of human beings in order to "see" into the body ... their equipment is built in!

This built-in sonar ability gives the cetaceans (dolphins and whales) the ability to sense many vibrations, not only the physiological state but the emotional aspects as well. They would be able to pick up on the varied vibrations of fear, depression, excitement, and sexual arousal, among other things. (The research with dolphins goes into this more extensively).

• Chapter Twenty-Six •

The Dolphin, Genius of the Sea

Since ancient times, the dolphin has been considered a special animal. For thousands of years dolphins have captured the imagination and heart of humankind. Legends and myths have been inspired by them, stories have been written about them, statues built of them, art and jewelry made in their image.

Plutarch the historian wrote about dolphins in A.D. 66 in his "Treatise on the Intelligence of Animals," in which he said that the dolphin possesses a gift that is longed for by the greatest of the world's philosophers—unselfish friendship. "It has no need of any man, yet is the friend of all men and has often given them great aid."

More than 2,500 years ago, the Greeks minted coins showing Poseidon's son riding, in spiritual communion, on the back of a dolphin that had saved his life. The ancient Greeks believed (even if too romantically and incorrectly) that dolphins were once "men who put on the form of fishes."

Who really knows for sure? Some fifteen million years ago, dolphins (and whales) walked on the land with four legs. The flippers that the dolphins use in the water for balance and direction evolved from the original front legs of the mammal. Over centuries of evolution, their air-breathing nostrils moved to become the blowhole at the top of the head. Modern dolphin skeletons reveal the vestige of a bone on either side of the tail, where hind legs once were.

In a February 1993 issue of *USA Today*, it was reported that fossils were found belonging to a "missing link" ancestor of the whale that walked on land and swam in the sea—fifty million years ago.

Discovered in Pakistan, the fossils support genetic studies showing that the closest cousins of modern whales are deer, cows, pigs, camels, and giraffes, among others. Paleontologist Hans Thewissen of Duke University in Durham, North Carolina, said, "Most animals first lived in the ocean and then moved to the shore. But there also were animals that walked on land and for some reason went back to the sea, and these were the whales."

Thewissen said that whales may have become fully oceangoing mammals forty-five million years ago. The first complete skeletons of whales that lived in the ocean date back to about forty million years old, and were discovered not far from the pyramids in Cairo.

For thousands of years men have testified that dolphins have aided them in locating fertile fishing grounds and even purposely driven fish into nets for a percentage of the take. For at least that long, stories have abounded that attest to dolphins saving lives, directing fogbound vessels out of dangerous reefs, and escorting shipwrecked and drowning sailors to dry land.

Throughout history there have been cooperative fishing efforts between the dolphins and many of the so-called primitive or aboriginal cultures of the world. These symbiotic relationships are still very much in evidence today. Natives in Australia, New Zealand, and the South Pacific, as well as the Amazon, Malaysia, and Indonesia tell of their joint ventures with dolphins.

Boto is the name the natives of the Amazon give to the dolphin we've named the Amazon River dolphin. Boto is considered sacred by the natives, who treat the dolphin with total respect. Boto comes to the fishermen's canoe when he hears paddles slapping the river's surface, and then drives fish ahead of him into the nets of the waiting natives.

The natives also tell how Boto protects swimmers from deadly piranhas and has been known to save swimmers whose boats have capsized by pushing them to shore.

The Irrawaddy dolphin that is native to the tropical Indo-Pacific waters, close to shore and in jungle rivers, also drives fish into the local fishermen's nets. Not far away, the natives tell of an eleven-year-old surfer who was recently swept out to sea in the Indian Ocean and miraculously rescued by a dolphin that chased away the sharks and stayed with the boy for four hours until he was rescued!

Our friend Lydia MacCarthy, an ethologist (one who studies animal behaviors), told us of her love for dolphins. Lydia has dedicated her life to working with and learning from the marvelous creatures. She agrees with Dr. Peter Morgane of The Worcester Foundation for Experimental Biology, of Worcester, Massachusetts, in his statement regarding dolphins and whales:

"We are dealing with special creatures with remarkably developed brains. Major riddles of nature and relations between species may indeed be answered by study of these brains. . . . They could have taught us much if we had only listened. Their kinship with man at the level of neurological development holds us in awe and fascination. . . . This is a resource and kinship that belongs to us all. Our very training and deepest feelings make us respect these wondrous creatures. Would that the brains of men could lead them to live in harmony with nature instead of ruthlessly plundering the seas (and jungles) that nurtured us."

MacCarthy and Morgane are both referring to the systematic stripping of the tropical rain forests and the insatiable greed that man has exhibited in polluting the coastal waters and destroying our planet's natural life-support system. Add to this the millions of dolphins (whales too) that have been killed because they were trapped in tuna nets by fishermen all over the world. These disturbing facts have added to the dwindling numbers of dolphins and whales—putting some on the endangered species list. In some cases, as with the spinner dolphin (the kind noted for their twisting leaps and frolicking), over 80 percent of a species have been wiped out.

With all the historical reverence for dolphins, it is only recently that research has discovered that the friendly, playful dolphin is highly intelligent. Some scientists consider the dolphin even more intelligent than the chimpanzee.

Some say a dolphin's brain is as large as or larger than a man's. But dolphin researcher Richard Connor says that the dolphin's brain is smaller than the human brain, yet roughly double the size of the great apes'.

"It is only in the past twenty years that researchers have been able to watch these large-brained mammals in the wild—what the hell are those animals doing out there with such big brains?" said Connor.

Connor, who has been working with dolphins at

Shark Bay, Australia, and biologist Randy Wells, who also has researched dolphins since 1982 at the University of California, Santa Cruz, and scientists observing dolphins in Sarasota, Florida, have each in their own separate ways documented a complex dolphin social system featuring lasting friendships, altruism, baby-sitting, cooperative defense, and elaborate communications.

Wells and his colleagues have determined that dolphins reside in communities of 100 or more that are stable over time and restricted to a specific home range. According to Lydia MacCarthy, recent studies of dolphin pods in coastal Hawaiian waters indicate that dolphins maintain a consistent limit to the size of their pod.

Lydia told us that when individual membership of the pod exceeds that limit, placing strain on the food supply and ecological balance of the pod's territory, some of the dolphins will swim off to establish new pods, thereby relieving the strain on the environment.

Other researchers say that because of the strong herding instinct that dolphins have, they live in schools of up to 1,000. Whatever the number of dolphins in a school or "pod" (the more correct grouping) actually might be, that is about the only piece of research that scientists seem to have differing views on.

Most other information gleaned from the study of dolphins matches up from researcher to researcher—and the data is piling up!

• Chapter Twenty-Seven •

A Whale of a Dolphin Story

Dolphins are actually members of the suborder of toothed whales *(Odontoceti)*. Most of us are not sure about the difference between dolphins and porpoises. But then throw in the fact that dolphins are whales, and it seems all too confusing. Then there is a game fish called dolphin that has nothing to do with the kind of dolphin or porpoise we are talking about here!

Purists refer to the members of the snouted families Delphinidae and Platanistidae as "dolphins." They use the term "porpoise" for the few species of Phocaenidae that lack a pronounced rostrum, or beak, and have spade-shaped rather than conical teeth. Most fishermen and some scientists call this kind porpoises.

It's probably safe to say that most people use the terms dolphin and porpoise interchangeably, and there's nothing wrong with that—unless you *are* a purist.

There is a somewhat varied opinion on how many species of dolphins or porpoises there are. Most agree there are about fifty or so. They are found in every ocean and even rivers of South America and Asia. They can vary in size from a dainty harbor porpoise, which is generally some 5 feet long, to the 25-foot, 7-ton *Orcinus orca*—the killer whale.

Dolphins . . . Smarter than the Average Bear . . . and That's No Fish Story!

The ability to use systems of abstract symbols, such as language, has been considered the exclusive domain of *Homo sapiens* and *was* the separating factor between man and beast; note the key word—*was!*

Recently, language researchers working with dolphins have shown that dolphins do have the cognitive skills to understand simple language. This includes concepts such as direction and the basic rules that govern language, such as the sequence of words. Also, dolphins have even started to *talk back*!

The ability to use language also includes the ability to conceive of images that aren't there, known as displacement. In the past, linguists and other researchers did not consider animals capable of imagination, which means using symbols to recall images.

For example, in one study done at the Kewalo Basin Marine Mammal Laboratory, at the University of Hawaii in Honolulu, dolphins were taught symbols for objects. When asked if a particular object was in the pool, the dolphin would have to look around and also recall what the symbol stood for. If that item was not in the pool, the dolphin would press a paddle that stands for no. In order to do this, the image had to be clearly in the dolphin's mind.

In fact, as far as memory goes, in tests at the University of Hawaii with dolphins and auditory memory (the ability to remember a specific tone), a dolphin easily outperformed another intelligent mammal—the human!

Symbolic communication is not confined among dolphins for use in an observation tank. In their native environment, dolphins consistently use language skills. Dolphins use sound signals to identify themselves to other dolphins as well as to communicate their emotional state and other information.

Dolphins have no vocal cords, but they do have a vocabulary of at least thirty-two distinct sounds (some scientists say up to 1,000), including clicks, whistles, barks, creaks, rasps, groans, and squeals. In addition, each dolphin has its own unique, distinctive voice.

The dolphin navigates by emitting sounds and picking up their echoes—sonar or echolocation. This has been known for some time. In 1950, in an experiment at the Oceanic Institute in Hawaii, blindfolded dolphins were able to determine the location, distance, size, and rigidity of an object by listening to the sound waves bouncing off it.

A dolphin's sonar radar is so acute that it can pick up sound underwater from 15 miles away—and can precisely locate an object as small as a vitamin pill at that distance.

Our human technology has only just begun to mimic the dolphin's sonar ability by using ultrasound. Echolocation (another word for this sonar ability) is three-dimensional. Vibrations bounce off the inside cavities of the body, guaging the echoes sounding from the heart, brain, kidneys, lungs, and so on.

In fact, dolphin researchers have told us that in "dolphin swims" with humans it is common for the dolphins to lead a pregnant woman away from the rest of the swimmers. The dolphins encircle her as if to protect her and act as dolphin midwives for the birth of a baby.

Many woman have first learned they were pregnant from the dolphins!

Sherry's friend and associate Dr. Daniel Fritz has been working with an experimental program (both in the United States and in the former Soviet Union) using dolphins throughout the entire pregnancy of a woman.

The woman and husband go into the dolphin tank or ocean on a nearly daily basis, swimming together. The dolphins, as well as doctors, are there for the birthing process—as midwives.

Initial research showed surprising results of calmer, more docile, intelligent babies. Born in this manner, they advanced at a much faster rate than babies born in the conventional way. Just why this appears true is not exactly clear yet, but the research continues.

More recently, scientists have developed Doppler echo technology. Dr. Alan Sutphen, a medical doctor who also works with cetaceans, says "that from our own Doppler echo we can hear the flow of blood through the microscopic capillaries of something like the human finger—sounding like a veritable roar."

This brings to mind that we are just learning how much the cetaceans actually "see." Interestingly, they can see equally well in or out of water—with their eyes. But with their "sonar eyes" they see a dimensional picture of everything that we can only now imagine because of our copying their inborn technology with ultrasounds, or sonograms.

A dolphin or a whale would be able to see right into you—entirely—if you were to enter the water with them. They would see your heart and hear your heartbeat, so they would know if you were excited or calm (an instant stress test). They would be able to detect a tumor, cancer, blocked arteries, your emotional state, if you were sad or happy, afraid or depressed, and so on.

In other words, if we could have a dolphin tell us what it saw, we'd have a complete physical.

Because of these amazing capabilities, dolphins are being researched in two very important and innovative ways. One is the continuing attempt at interspecies communications, learning a common language in order for humans and dolphins to "talk." The second is the use of dolphins with underprivileged and handicapped children. The results so far are amazing.

• Chapter Twenty-Eight •

Dolphin Communication

The man who is credited by most for being the scientist who literally ushered in an era of animal communication and language research is Dr. John C. Lilly. Dr. Lilly, a neurophysiologist and psychoanalyst, believed that dolphins were extremely intelligent and that they possessed an "immensely complex" natural language.

Lilly was struck by the size and complexity of the dolphin brain, "They [dolphins] are here, waiting for us to grow up and maturely communicate," he said.

Citing that the dolphin had unusually large "silent associational areas" (heavily fissured cortical regions where intellectual capacity such as language presumably resides), he was convinced that dolphins were capable of talking.

Dr. Lilly began his intense research with dolphins in 1955, and his approach to communicating with the dolphins was based on a method of teaching the dolphins

English by talking to them repetitively and taping their responses. He would then attempt to slow down the speed of the dolphin messages to decipher them.

A Teenage Pioneer's Invention Launches Dolphin Research

A mutual friend and associate of ours, Dr. G. Patrick Flanagan, was instrumental in the earliest attempts at communicating with dolphins. In 1959, Patrick Flanagan, at the age of fourteen, received a patent for his invention, the neurophone. The neurophone was a "listening" device utilizing an entirely different process of hearing—not through the ears. His device and its improvement, the neurophone II, has been used in amazing breakthrough technology that will enable deaf people to hear and blind people to see.

Patrick became actively involved in man-dolphin communications for the Office of Naval Research. Vice-president in charge of research for Listening, Inc., Patrick was under contract with the U.S. Naval Ordnance Test Station in China Lake, California. They worked with dolphins in a lagoon, near the University of Hawaii facility on Coconut Island off Oahu, Hawaii. In conjunction with Steve Moshier, Patrick designed a computer that translates human speech into Dolphin Language, and Dolphin Language into English. The translator detects human speech forms and translates them into a whistle language using sounds normally used by dolphins.

The translator's mate, the DMT (dolphin-man translator) performs the reverse function, making sounds like human speech from dolphin whistle inputs.

Through the same program, Patrick and team invented an acoustical generator called the Sondol, or the Sonic Dolphin. The Sondol produces pulses very similar to those produced by dolphins in echolocation. Sondol has been tested by human subjects and is being used to aid the blind in sensing the environment and to the scuba diver for perception in murky waters.

Evaluation of dolphins signals and sounds has given us some understanding of their language. Each dolphin has its own "signature" whistle, which is equivalent to its name. Dolphins can also imitate the signatures of other dolphins. Combining another dolphin's signature whistle with its own, a dolphin would be in effect saying, "Hey, Brad, it's me Sherry—over here" (if the dolphins' names were Brad and Sherry!). The length and pitch of a dolphin's whistle tone adds further information.

The dolphin's sonic repertoire seems to include emotional signals as well. A rising and falling birdlike cry would be the dolphin's cry for "Help!"

Dr. Peter Tyack, a scientist at Woods Hole Oceanographic Institution, says, "As far as we know, humans and marine mammals like dolphins are the only animals that modify what they say in response to what they hear."

There are other fascinating projects around the country that have had phenomenal success in working with dolphin communications.

At the Kewalo Basin Marine Mammal Laboratory, in Hawaii, psychologist Louis Herman, director of the lab, became interested in dolphin communications in the 1970s, when studies of language in champanzees and other great apes were receiving a great deal of attention. He wanted to parallel this type of research using dolphins. He calls the dolphins the "cognitive cousins" of the great apes.

Dr. Herman designed two artificial languages to test dolphin comprehension. One was teaching them a vocabulary of hand signals, the other an acoustic language composed of computer-generated, whistlelike sounds that are broadcast into the tank through an underwater speaker (using similar equipment to that described above).

The two initial dolphins Ake and Phoenix each learned approximately fifty "words." Each gesture (hand signal) or auditory sign stands for either an object (like a ball) or an action (such as fetch) or a location or direction (such as under).

Dr. Herman is elated over the possibilities the success of these experiments opens up. In recombining the words the dolphins have in their vocabulary, more than 1,000 different sentences have been given, each one eliciting an unlearned, unrehearsed response!

Dr. Herman and his staff also wanted to find out if the dolphins could understand and master word order and syntax as well. As described earlier, they found out they can. By using the skill called displacement— retaining an image of what the word stands for and recalling it even if the object is not visible.

Dr. Herman and his team have now designed an experiment that will allow the dolphins to say more. A large board displaying sixteen different symbols will be placed on the floor of the dolphin tank with symbols selected from the dolphin's vocabulary. A television monitor will display the symbol the dolphin selects by pushing a paddle under that symbol. The TV screen keeps track of what the dolphin says in a visual way, so the dolphin and trainer can see what is said.

Dr. Herman makes clear that his goal is to "map out the many dimensions of the dolphins' intellect, so that we can come to an understanding of what it's like cognitively to be a dolphin."

Teachers of the Sea

At the Dolphin Research Center on Florida's Grassy Key, David Nathanson, a psychologist, is pioneering an innovative program with dolphins and handicapped children. Dr. Nathanson's two projects—using Atlantic bottlenose dolphins to increase cognition of mentally retarded children, and using nonhumans (pet therapy) to increase learning—have been highly successful.

One example of a typical interaction occurred with a ten-year-old boy named Robert, who was profoundly handicapped. Dr. Nathanson and the boy's family urged Robert to throw a board that had a line drawing of a car into the pool where the dolphin was. Robert sat on the side of the pool, dangling his feet in the water.

The dolphin picked up the board, carrying it in his mouth to Dr. Nathanson. Robert watched intently. Then the researcher took the board from the dolphin and held it up, showing Robert and saying, "This is a car, can you say car?"

Hesitating, Robert suddenly burst out excitedly, "Car!" All who were present burst out into applause and elated cheers. That was the first word Robert ever spoke—in ten years!

Other children in Dr. Nathanson's project had various disabilities such as Downs syndrome. Like Robert, the children identified and pronounced the names of objects represented on simple picture boards.

Dr. Nathanson said that "the children learned anywhere from one-and-a-half times to ten times more, in fact. That's between 50 and a 1,000 percent increase—when they were exposed to dolphins." The children were given the choice of petting, feeding, swimming, or kissing the dolphin. The dolphins were given fish—all rewards that add to the success of the interaction.

There are other programs that work with dolphins in similar ways. In Connecticut, a researcher named Patricia St. John has been integrating dolphin therapy with autistic children. In the Florida Keys, a group called "Dolphin Plus" has had positive results using Atlantic bottlenose dolphins with autistic children.

An organization called the International Human–Animal Interaction Organization, or the Delta Society, is attempting to coordinate other programs along these lines. They have said there seems to be a new trend among scientists toward using animals to help the handicapped.

Some interesting facts have come out of the various research programs about dolphins.

Some researchers believe that beluga whales and other cetaceans might exist in a permanent alpha state—the ideal, relaxed state, where creativity is heightened. Cetaceans can never really "fall asleep" because they have to consciously take a breath of air. Their breathing is not autonomic like ours. If they should happen to doze off—they die.

Researchers think that the cetaceans (dolphins and whales) use only one hemisphere of their brain at a time, resting the other half. In the wild, scientists have observed pods of dolphins in which all those on one side swim with one eye closed. Those swimming guard on the other side of the pod have the opposite eye closed. Even though they are resting one side of their brain, they seem keenly aware of their surroundings.

Dolphin Rx for a Tummy Ache

When a dolphin gets a tummy ache, it gets a whopper, because it has two stomachs. Some scientists suggest that because of certain behavior patterns and blood-serum analysis, before sliding back into the sea some fifty million years ago, the ancestral cetacean shared dim evolutionary linkage with today's barnyard ruminants.

Truly, dolphins are subject to human ailments. They do suffer from ulcers of the stomachs. And the Rx, or prescription is: one gallon of ground fish and Maalox broth, by tube, three times daily!

Other common ailments dolphins experience are pneumonia, parasites, and skin problems. They are very susceptible to stress. In fact, that is what most doctors think leads to their stomach ulcers—just like us!

"Dolphins also concentrate salts in their kidneys in a similar way as camels," said Dr. Sam Houston Ridgway, a research veterinarian at the U.S. Naval Ocean Systems Center (NOSC) in San Diego. His opinion is that cetaceans seem to "sleep" with one eye open and half of the brain awake only two or three hours a day. The jury seems still to be out on the "sleep" of cetaceans.

Music Appreciation—for Sea Mammals

It also seems that the sea mammals (seals included) like music. Many experiments have been conducted by such people as Roger Payne of the Lincoln, Massachusetts, Whale Conservation Institute, who recorded intricate humpback whale lullabies.

Sherry's friend and associate Paul Winter became increasingly aware of environmental issues in the early 1970s. He joined Greenpeace expeditions, playing his saxophone in the waters off the coast of British Columbia. Soon he found that his raft was surrounded by humpback whales.

"Just listening to them breathe was like the earth itself come alive," he said. The whales and dolphins seemed to "sing along" and be entranced with the music. He began recording and integrating whale, dolphin, and wolf sounds into his own recordings.

Two of his best-selling albums with the living music of the animals answering the call of Winter's saxophone are *Callings* and *Common Ground*. *Callings* was made in cooperation with fifteen species of sea mammals, from humpback whales to seals.

In 1976, Paul formed a nonprofit organization designed to acknowledge the living sounds of nature and wild beings and to reawaken the natural resources of harmony and rhythm within people through their participation in music making. Such notables as Dizzy Gillespie, Dave Brubeck, Judy Collins, and John Denver have been on the foundation's advisory board.

The Paul Winter Consort gives benefit concerts throughout the world. The proceeds from the concerts and albums are shared with the animals through various conservation groups across the United States.

• Chapter Twenty-Nine •

Alice the Porpoise Joins the U.S. Navy

While she was blindfolded Alice was able to find her way quickly and safely through an underwater maze. She could whistle and talk, and she possessed the ability to operate sonar better than anyone else in the U.S. Navy.

These accomplishments are all the more amazing when one considers that Alice was a porpoise who joined the navy in the 1960s.

For decades now, the navy has been very curious about the ability of porpoises to navigate so well underwater. The Office of Naval Research [ONR] hopes to be able to find out just how the sea mammals are able to perform their miraculous feats in order to help perfect their own underwater weapons and guidance systems. Since at least the late 1940s, a great deal of scientific interest has been stimulated by such underwater wizards as Alice.

Great excitement was aroused in the scientific community when it was determined that porpoises communicated with one another in a systematic language not yet understood by humans.

Alice was 7 feet long and weighed 300 pounds. Like most porpoises, Alice was amusing, intelligent, very loyal; and she proved to be a very willing partner in all the tests that pioneering scientists in the area of porpoise research could think up.

Alice's landlocked home was a large saltwater tank at the University of California in Los Angeles. She swam swiftly, performed her duties cheerfully, and amazed the scientists with the ease in which she navigated the underwater obstacle courses they had constructed.

The extraordinary intellect of the porpoise has prompted the use of the aquatic mammals as featured performers in the world of animal show business, and the cooperative sea dwellers entertain visitors at various marineland shows and through reruns of the popular television show *Flipper*.

Many years ago it was observed that among their many other talents, the porpoise has an uncanny skill at navigation. Alice became the willing "guineaporpoise" in numerous tests devised by navy scientists. Among other goals, the researchers wished to be able to duplicate her great mobility and speed.

Time after time Alice would swim around her saltwater tank at UCLA, bypassing dozens of obstacles to find the designated target.

Eventually, some of the scientists began to suspect that Alice did not navigate solely with the use of her eyes, so they blindfolded her and sent her through the maze again. The patient porpoise obliged them by repeating her swim through the obstacle course without a miss—and once again hit the target with her beaklike nose. Alice had been navigating by the use of her natural sonar.

Technically, sonar is an apparatus that detects the presence and location of underwater objects with the use of sound waves. Much like an echo coming from a faraway hill, sound waves are sent out from the sonar apparatus and the sensitive device picks up the echoes, or returning waves, from any solid object near the receiver. Among other applications of the process, sonar is used in antisubmarine warfare.

Navy scientists were surprised and perhaps a trifle embarrassed when they discovered that Alice's natural sonar was superior to any that their sophisticated technology had been able to produce.

The porpoise's sonar has two distinct advantages over the sonar of human science: first, the porpoise does not need to use pure tones, but can use mixed frequencies for the location of objects underwater. Second, the porpoise focuses its sonar beam, a feat that scientists keep trying to achieve.

• Chapter Thirty •

Top Secret! (Just Declassified): Secret Service Dolphins

"C lassified" is the answer just about everyone gets when asking the U.S. Navy *how* they use dolphins. For many years, in fact, the navy has denied the training and use of dolphins for military projects. It has only been fairly recently that representatives speaking for the U.S. Navy have publicly admitted their use in the Gulf War, for example.

The navy confessed that their dolphins were in the Gulf detecting mines, finding sunken torpedoes, and locating Iranian frogmen. A spokesperson at the Naval Ocean Systems Center in San Diego said, "Dolphins can pick out objects at a distance with incredible accuracy; their sonar system is better than any radar."

Another official said that about half a dozen navy-trained porpoises were sent to Vietnam to "test their transportability over long distances, their adaptability—tests you simply can't make in a laboratory." The navy wanted to know if the dolphins would be capable of performing detection and surveillance functions under the difficult circumstances of a foreign, tropical environment, in a bay that is full of warships and debris.

Dolphins have many skills and talents the navy hoped to explore. Some of the questions the navy hoped to learn from dolphins were: do dolphins have habits that would be beneficial for the navy to use? Could the navy develop a dolphin-type sonar system? Could the navy employ dolphins to reduce hazards to humans in diving tasks?

We know the navy must have answers to these and other questions by now, since they have actively been researching and training dolphins for over 30 some years (starting in the 1950s).

In a 1979 issue of *National Geographic,* Harris B. Stone, director of the research and development and in charge of the Navy's porpoise work for the Chief of Naval Operations, was quoted as saying: "We have employed porpoises in open-ocean work. We are making use of their remarkable sensory capabilities. But we are not about to telegraph how and where and what they're used for to a potential adversary by discussing it."

That has been the general attitude of the navy ever since. This certainly makes sense. None of us wants to jeopardize the security of our nation; but we guess because dolphins have become so beloved in the eyes of the public that we feel a protective concern for them.

Stone said, "The navy has never used porpoises for anything that would harm either the animals or any human being. To me the 'killer dolphin' story is ludicrous." Edward J. Linehan, in his article for *National Geographic,* "The Trouble with Dolphins," had been shown a carbon dioxide dart that fits into a black plastic sheath strapped onto the dolphin.

The navy developed the dart gun to protect divers against sharks. It is now available at dive shops around the country for underwater divers for the same purpose. Mr. Stone was illustrating his opinion of how a James Bond thriller was created by the media and such to create a scenario of explosives, gas cartridges in lances, and guns strapped to the backs of dolphins who were to seek the enemy and fire—often at their own risk—from a simple shark protection device.

There are other stories from credible sources that experimentation with the dolphins involves many other things potentially lethal to them as well.

Incredibly, at a 750-foot depth in the ocean (a depth that would be dangerous or deadly to humans), a dolphin's rib cage collapses, driving all the air from its lungs. This flexibility would prevent nitrogen from being absorbed into the dolphin's bloodstream, with the advantage of not getting the bends, as human divers do.

In experiments to find out how deep a dolphin can go, amazing depths of at least 1,700 feet have been reached—out of a hoped-for 2,500 feet.

A leading Washington military analyst said recently, "It's silly for the navy to deny they're using dolphins in the Gulf War.

"They've trained over 240 animals at secret facilities in Honolulu, Key West, and San Diego. They've published an incredible 200 papers on the dolphins' many outstanding abilities to help humans with underwater tasks."

He went on to say that it just stands to reason that with all that effort, money, and training, why wouldn't they take advantage of the top-secret dolphins to help in a war situation such as the Gulf War?

The dolphins have at least one devoted advocate fighting for their cause. Richard O'Barry, the trainer of the most famous dolphin (or dolphins, we should say, trained to play the one and only), Flipper, star of the long-running television series "Flipper."

Our friend Kai King interviewed O'Barry for *Chal-*

lenge magazine, summer 1990 issue. O'Barry expressed the thought he has spent more hours than anybody working with dolphins. For seven years, "twenty-four hours a day," he said, he swam and lived with the dolphins. He grew to view dolphins as a "nation of people," not fish, and he thinks of himself as their lone spokesperson.

O'Barry is against the sea parks, calling them "abusement" parks. He stresses the fact that about half of the dolphins die in captivity.

The key point to him is that rather than ambassadors, a term the oceanariums like to use in referring to dolphins, the dolphins are a whole different breed of dolphins that humans have created—domesticated dolphins.

O'Barry said there are 352 dolphins in captivity in America and that he has a list of every single one of them, as their adoptive guardian angel of sorts.

O'Barry said a large percentage of the dolphins spend their lives in concrete tanks inside buildings that aren't located by the ocean. When they are born in captivity, these dolphins never see the sky or swim in a real ocean to experience life as it should be for a dolphin.

That is a very sad dilemma. We as humans have domesticated many animals, changing the "natural" plot of their evolution perhaps. It seems that a dog or cat is no worse off for becoming the household pet. Another factor has entered into consideration now that so much research is being done with other animals, such as birds (parrots), and chimpanzees.

Discovering that certain of these animals are so intelligent, beyond most of our wildest thoughts—what do we do next? We have often puzzled over whether it's fair to keep a bird locked up in a cage, when it seems it was born to fly in an unlimited sky.

We rationalize that these birds are being bred for this pet-purpose, and as we mentioned in the section on birds, they make better pets when they are bred in captivity. But does that alter a species and limit it—or give it new horizons and opportunities, and most importantly, the gift of love?

It might make a difference when a species such as the dolphin is as smart or nearly as smart as—or smarter than—we are! Are we holding them captive?

Dr. John C. Lilly predicted in his early work with dolphins: "Within the next decade or two, the human species will establish communication with another species: non-human, alien, possibly extraterrestrial, more probably marine; but definitely highly intelligent, perhaps even intellectual."

O'Barry makes the point that we spend millions or billions of dollars to search for extraterrestrial life in space, when all of the time we have intelligent life in the sea—the dolphins. And what do we do but cage them up, kill millions of them in tuna nets, and make circus clowns out of them.

Well, even if he seems a bit cynical, one cannot help but think that there must be some "happy medium," some useful compromises.

There are many programs springing up that are allowing the dolphins free range in their native habitat. The navy has gone with what they refer to as "open-sea release," and "swim with the dolphins in their natural state out-at-sea" type opportunities are available.

The Dolphin Research Center has sixteen Atlantic bottlenose dolphins and allow swimming with the dolphins—all in a beautiful natural setting. O'Barry heads The Dolphin Project in Coconut Grove, Florida. His boat takes people 40 miles out to sea and plays music underwater to swim to. The dolphins just come naturally and swim in a water ballet with the human participants.

Many alternatives such as these will continue to take

the dolphin's best interest and protect it. But what of the military?

A federal court settlement was recently approved, which is a victory for dolphin rights. On May 3, 1990, in a lawsuit against the U.S. Navy's use of dolphins to guard nuclear submarines at Bangor, Washington, was also a victory for Richard O'Barry. The settlement between environmentalists and the navy states that the navy must:

1. get approval before capturing dolphins
2. must do an environmental impact study before using dolphins in any way.

This move "will for the first time make the navy live within the guidelines of the 1972 Marine Mammal Protection Act like everyone else," said O'Barry.

The navy has had an estimated 143 dolphins according to some, over the last 15 years, and more than 83 are dead. The use of warm-water dolphins in the cold water off Washington State was a death sentence to dolphins, O'Barry said.

On June 13, 1990, the *Miami Herald* reported the arrest of Richard O'Barry and "Inside Edition" reporter Craig Rivera, on charges of violating national security. They were released after handing over all the film shot of a pair of navy-trained dolphins held in pens at Truman Annex Training Facility. O'Barry said the Key West dolphins were being used to patrol a Trident nuclear submarine.

In a book about animal intelligence, we must consider ourselves—the human. How "humane" are we with a war consciousness that has plagued the earth since the beginning? We can champion activists like O'Barry and Greenpeace, or even the sea parks for opening our eyes and thoughts somewhat about the mysterious sea creatures; but we have a long way to go with other issues equally important—like how we treat our fellow "humans." Education is always the start!

More data emerges from sensitive and caring researchers such as that in the fascinating book The *Lives of Whales and Dolphins*, by Richard Connor, Ph.D. with Dawn Peterson. Connor says that dolphins have been seen to use tools in the imitation of divers. An intimate look at over seventy-five species of whales and dolphins describes many stages of how these fascinating and intelligent mammals learn, communicate, play, reproduce, and even fight and express emotions. In one experience they describe how a baby right whale has "temper tantrums when he wants milk from his mama whale and mama says *no*!"

So, as many scientists and researchers collaborate in their fascination with the inner space of our oceans' life and continue to explore the mystery, the beauty, and the intelligence of not only the dolphins and whales but the harmonious interchange of other life down under, we may learn much more of how these awe-inspiring creatures are interlinked with our lives and existence.

Note: The International Whaling Commission banned commercial whaling beginning in 1986.

Even since then, it has been reported that Iceland, Japan, and Norway have been whaling and/or buying and selling hundreds of tons of whale meat—often under various "scientific" guises. For more information contact: Greenpeace, P.O. Box 3720, Washington, D.C. 20007.

• Chapter Thirty-One •

The Primates: How Intelligent Are Our Nearest Evolutionary Cousins?

Lindsay Schmidt, an Australian sheep rancher, spotted smoke coming from one of the trucks in the traveling circus and just naturally did what any decent man would do: he put out the fire that was smoldering inside the vehicle.

The owners of the circus were extremely grateful to the resourceful rancher, and they wished to reward him for his quick thinking. Unfortunately, they didn't really have any money, so they offered Schmidt a monkey that was only a few weeks old. Schmidt accepted the tiny bundle and straightaway named him Johnnie.

Friends say that they had never seen any two creatures bond faster than the rancher and the monkey. It was as if Lindsay had become Johnnie's father.

A practical man, Schmidt saw no reason why he needed a human hired hand on the ranch now that he had his "son" Johnnie to help him out.

Johnnie had no complaints about life on the ranch. It

wasn't long before he was opening bales and spreading hay for the sheep, tossing grain for the chickens, and helping his "pa" to herd the livestock.

Even more amazing, when he had attained his full growth, Johnnie sat confidently behind the wheel of Schmidt's tractor. Not only could Johnnie expertly steer the farm vehicle around rocks and trees, but he was also capable of starting the machine, shifting gears, and applying the brakes.

The May 15, 1964, issue of *Life* magazine recounted the remarkable symbiotic lifestyle of Schmidt and his Johnnie. The two had their division of labor down to the point where Schmidt would pack the lunch bags with their meals, but Johnnie would be responsible for collecting all the scraps and litter and disposing of them properly.

Jack the Baboon Was an Efficient Switchman on the Railroad

Perhaps even more remarkable than Johnnie's prowess at the wheel of a farm tractor is the story from South Africa from the mid-1800s that tells of the baboon named Jack who efficiently controlled railway switches.

It seems that when James Wide, a signalman at the Vitenhage Tower on the Johannesburg–Pretoria Railway, had the misfortune of losing both of his legs in a railway accident, he beseeched the officials not to cast him off into a charity ward. He insisted that his pet baboon could assume his job of operating the railway switches.

How could Wide make such a preposterous claim?

Because, he told the railway authorities, Jack had already been assisting him with such domestic duties as pumping water from the well, weeding and watering the vegetable garden, and keeping their cottage clean.

For nine years, Jack sat at the switches in the Vitenhage Tower and masterfully operated the sets of levers as the trains roared by the station. He pushed and pulled the levers that set the signals and operated the controls that opened or closed the switches. In all that time, he never once made a mistake that caused a mishap.

Jack was officially placed on the payroll of the Johannesburg–Pretoria Railway. He was paid 20 cents a day and half a bottle of beer on Saturdays.

Harvard University's Dr. Irven De Vore has spent many years studying primate behavior for clues that might enrich our perspective of human evolution. In an interview in a recent issue of *Omni* magazine, Dr. De Vore commented that scientists have recently discovered certain behavior traits in chimpanzees that even a decade ago no responsible academician would have attributed to our hominid ancestors.

"Jane Goodall's study sites at Gombe, and Toshisada Nishida's site in the mountains of Tanzania indicate that chimps use tools and that males will occasionally surround and kill young animals," he pointed out by way of illustration.

"Female chimps in the Tai Forest are expert tool makers, using a variety of hardwoods to crack different kinds of nuts. They systematically cache rare stones, fetching them when a hard-nut tree is in fruit."

Sheba's Days Are Numbered

In 1987, psychologist Sarah T. Boysen of Ohio State University reported that Sheba, one of the chimpanzees in her laboratory, had learned to count and to add small numbers of objects or Arabic numerals.

According to Boysen, Sheba had first learned to select a round placard with a corresponding number of metal disks attached in response to being shown one, two, or three food items. The talented chimp then mastered how to do the same thing with placards containing the Arabic numerals 1, 2, and 3.

"When shown individual numbers on a video screen, [Sheba] was usually able to select the corresponding number on a placard ... indicating comprehension of the number symbols," reported *Science News* (Vol. 134, no. 9). "Upon presentation of one, two, or three common household items, Sheba demonstrated the same number-labeling skill. Placards with the numbers 0 and 4 were then added to Sheba's repertoire."

A new experiment to test Sheba's abilities was devised in which she was allowed to move among three displays in a laboratory room—a tree stump, a food bin, and a plastic dish. At each site she was asked to select the correct Arabic numeral for the number of oranges that the researchers had placed there.

According to Boysen, Sheba chose the correct sum in the various experiments about 80 percent of the time. In her opinion, the chimp's abilities compared favorably with the "rudimentary counting strategies observed among preschool children."

Can We Teach the Primates to Speak Good English?

Scientific endeavors to teach primates to speak is hardly a new research project. Early in this century, there were a number of pioneer researchers who earnestly tried to teach chimpanzees to speak English or Russian. After years of consistent failure, most scientists concluded that as intelligent as certain primates may be, the language barrier could never be broken.

It was during the late 1960s, that time of expanded

social consciousness and individual awareness, that some determined laboratory researchers discovered that they could achieve greater success in communicating with primates if they utilized visual signs rather than speech.

By 1971, Beatrice and R. Allen Gardner had employed simplified American Sign Language to teach Washoe, a young female chimpanzee, to "speak" with 150 hand gestures.

It was as if the time had suddenly come for successful studies in primate communication, for about the same time as the Gardners were signing with Washoe, psychologist David Premack was using plastic chips to talk with a chimp named Sarah; and psychologist Duane Rumbaugh was teaching Lana, a bright chimpanzee, to communicate by touching geometric symbols on a computer keyboard.

During the anything-can-happen 1970s, a number of enthusiastic researchers concluded that their experiments provided strong evidence that certain intelligent members of the various primate groups could be taught to combine words to express thoughts in a manner similar to that of human children.

However, by the dawn of the 1970s, serious academic critics, as well as some of the pioneer researchers themselves, began to evaluate the data a great deal more strenuously.

For example, did a conversing chimp really understand the difference between signing "Me eat orange" and "Orange eat me"?

There was an enormous distinction between being able to memorize a number of signs, as it appeared the primates had done quite successfully, and actually developing the ability to master grammatical rules that would enable an intelligent communicator to structure an endless variety of meaningful sentences from a vast pool of words.

Other critics pointed out that while there seemed little question that various primates had learned to associate certain signs with certain objects and to link them correctly in return for rewards the question remained whether such actions were due to anything more than the classic training method of conditioned response.

And there were no researchers, regardless of how meticulous their methods, who could prove that a primate could conceive of the *idea* of a banana when it produced the correct sign to earn a banana as a reward. By the early 1980s, it appeared as though the various projects of teaching primates to communicate had fallen into academic disrepute.

Duane Rumbaugh and Sue Savage-Rumbaugh "kept the faith," however, and persevered with a program on teaching primates symbolic representation, a project that they had begun during the late 1970s at the Language Research Center, a joint venture of the Yerkes center and Georgia State University. Breakthrough research with two chimps named Sherman and Austin subsequently led to the discovery of the remarkable Kanzi.

Since about 1985 Kanzi, a pygmy chimp protégé of the Language Research Center near Atlanta, Georgia, has been regarded as the primate who has achieved the most advanced linguistic abilities ever documented in an animal. While the ability of common chimpanzees to comprehend language became less clear to the careful scrutiny of scientific research, psychologist Duane Rumbaugh of Georgia State University in Atlanta felt qualified to state that the pygmy chimpanzee was capable of learning English words and short sentences without specific training.

Together with his colleague Sue Savage-Rumbaugh,

Rumbaugh directed research with Kanzi, who was consistently able to identify objects in his environment and to engage in certain behavior that corresponded to 149 of 194 words.

In order to keep their research methods under as strict controls as possible, Kanzi heard the words through headphones, so the "caregivers" interacting with him would not be aware of which word was being tested by the psychologists.

Kanzi repeatedly demonstrated his understanding of simple sentences of at least three words. If Kanzi might be told, "I hid the surprise by my foot," he would immediately approach the speaker and lift his or her foot to reveal the treat.

In the researchers' evaluation of Kanzi's capabilities, the chimp was not as adroit at the use of symbols on a keyboard to communicate his requests as he was accomplished at human language comprehension.

The psychologists observed, however, that Kanzi often placed pairs of symbols together in novel ways. In phrasing his requests, the chimp usually placed action words before objects. If, for example, he wanted to tease a caregiver with a balloon and initiate a playful fight, he would press the symbols for "keepway balloon."

Sue Savage-Rumbaugh told *The New York Times* for the June 25, 1985 issue, that in his motor skills and his interest in competitive games, Kanzi "was like a seven- or eight-year-old boy. He'd like to have boys around to play tackle football."

Duane Rumbaugh acknowledged that Kanzi acquired some grammatical ordering rules from those researchers who worked with him, but he believed that the intelligent chimp had developed other ordering rules on his own. In Rumbaugh's scientific assessment, "The pygmy chimpanzee species can understand substantial amounts of speech. This was unanticipated and came about with no specific training."

By March 1991, *Discover* magazine reported that Kanzi was capable of understanding some 650 sentences.

Even with such a remarkable track record, such projects as those conducted by Rumbaugh and Savage-Rumbaugh remain controversial among their scientific peers.

When Harvard sociobiologist Dr. Irven De Vore was asked his opinion of the great apes that had been taught to "speak," he told an interviewer for *Omni* magazine that while he was intrigued by such enterprises, he had always had serious doubts about their possible success, "because the great enlarged areas of the human brain that facilitate information processing and the subtle use of the vocal apparatus are simply not that large in chimpanzees.

"It's remarkable that chimps have progressed as far as they have toward linguistic communication, and most of the earlier studies are now viewed with considerable skepticism.

"We are just beginning to appreciate the complexity and subtlety of the chimpanzee mind and behavior. . . . It's an anthropocentric pretense to insist that they meet a human measure to communicate in a modern language."

Most evenings, according to Savage-Rumbaugh, when Kanzi is permitted a break from his studies, he asks to watch television or videos. A documentary on Jane Goodall studying chimpanzees in Africa is one of Kanzi's favorite videos. Others are the movies *Every Which Way But Loose* and *Any Which Way You Can*, pairing Clint Eastwood with the orangutan Clyde, and the epic adventure *Quest for Fire*, which portrays primitive humans seeking the life-giving warmth of fire.

Kanzi signals his request for that film by punching the symbols for "campfire" and "TV".

Eight Years among the Orangutans of the Borneo Jungles

After eight years of living with the orangutans of Borneo, Dr. Birute M. F. Galdikas, adjunct associate professor of anthropology at the University of New Mexico, commented that she and her husband, Rod Brindamour, had amassed more than 12,000 hours of observation that served to tear down part of the veil that had long shrouded orangutan life in the wild.

And after rearing their own child in close association with baby orangutans, they felt prepared to be able to make some remarkable insights and comparisons with these endangered great apes. "Along with chimpanzees and gorillas, they are humankind's closest living relatives and, after humans, the most intelligent of all land animals," Dr. Galdikas stated.

After the first five years of living with the orangutans, Dr. Galdikas found that she had reached the point where the line between human and ape was becoming increasingly blurred.

"Sometimes I felt as though I were surrounded by wild, unruly children in orange suits who had not yet learned their manners," she said [*National Geographic*, June 1980]. "They used tools, liked to wear bits and pieces of clothing, loved to indulge in junk food and candies, were insatiably curious, wanted constant affection and attention, expressed emotions such as anger and embarrassment in a manner seemingly very similar to human beings."

With her knowledge of laboratory studies being conducted back in the United States, which indicated that apes could use sign language and were capable of complex reasoning, Dr. Galdikas found herself beginning to doubt whether orangutans "were all that different from human beings."

But with the birth of their son, Binti Paul Galdikas Brindamour, she had the unique opportunity to compare the development of Princess, a one- to two-year-old orangutan female infant that she was hand-raising, with the development of "Bin."

A one-year-old orangutan is content to cling to its mother, and being extremely food oriented, displays very little interest in things other than those it might chew.

Bin, at the same age, was food oriented only when hungry, was fascinated by objects and implements and with watching others manipulate them.

"Another major difference," she noted, "was that Bin babbled constantly, while Princess was silent except when squealing."

Dr. Galdikas was intrigued to discover that "many of the traits associated with the emergence of humankind were already expressed in Bin's development before the age of one: bipedal locomotion, food sharing, tool using, speech."

The expression of such traits sharply differentiated Bin from an orangutan of the equivalent age. Dr. Galdikas knew from her work with older orangutans that the apes were capable of such behavior at a later age, but none of the humanlike traits would ever be developed as fully as in a maturing human child.

Continuing to be fascinated with the reports she heard of scientists successfully teaching sign language to laboratory chimps and gorillas, Dr. Galdikas theorized that by teaching orangutans sign language in their native habitat, scientists might find out "what was important to them, rather than to us."

After a time, Dr. Galdikas was fortunate in obtaining

the skills and expertise of Gary Shapiro, who had already spent two years teaching symbolic communication to a laboratory orangutan and who had worked with Washoe, the first of the signing chimpanzees.

She had little doubt that Sugito, one of the older orangutans, would be capable of learning sign language. He was already in the habit of handing her the key to the storeroom when he wanted food.

Unfortunately, Sugito had already become a murderer. To their great sorrow and disappointment, Dr. Galdikas and her husband discovered that he had been killing infants of his kind when he jealously feared that they were robbing him of human affection. And now, because he had been reared as much like a human as possible, Sugito was at the stage of his orangutan development where all other males were viewed as rivals to be attacked or avoided. Since Sugito did not distinguish between human and orangutan males, Shapiro could not get close enough to him to teach him a single aspect of symbolic sign language.

Shapiro was, however, able to teach American Sign Language to Rinnie, a bright, responsive female, who within weeks was asking for more food or additional contact by using signs. Princess was able to use sign language in a much broader sense, and she and Bin were soon communicating regularly through signing.

Dr. Galdikas insists that their eight-year study in the orangutan's natural habitat in their Bornean environment represents "only a good beginning," and she admits that she still finds it very difficult to say how close the relationship is between human beings and orangutans.

According to Dr. Irven De Vore, we humans stand in relation to the chimpanzee and other hominids as "second cousins who are descended from common great-grandparents."

Stressing that there never was a "missing link" between humans and the primates, he said in a recent *Omni* magazine interview, "Nevertheless, when you examine the remains of the earliest australopithecines . . . you are looking at a creature three to four million years old that comes amazingly close to combining human and ape traits."

The sense of wonder over who we really are as human beings and what our true place in the universe might truly be predates history. When the psalmist directed the query "What is man that Thou are mindful of him?" to the heavens, we can be certain that such a cry for meaningful answers had been sent toward the stars many times prior to his plaintive utterance.

It is our earnest hope that we will direct our sense of wonder with equal fervor toward achieving a deeper, more respectful understanding of the place of animals in our universe than our species has endeavored to comprehend and to practice in the past.

AN INTELLIGENCE TEST FOR YOUR PET

If your pet was easily housebroken rate it a 10. If it required several failed attempts before success, give it a 5. Subtract *two* points for each "accident" after you thought it was housebroken.

If your pet always listens calmly when you speak to it and gives you its full attention, give it a 10. If it is attentive *most* of the time, give it a 7. *Some* of the time rates a 4. *Hardly ever* scores a 1.

Does your pet respond readily when you call its name or give it a command? Then give it a 10. *Most* of the time rates a 7. *Sometimes* gains a 4. *Hardly ever* rates a 1.

If your pet has a long attention span when you are teaching it new commands, reward it with a 10. *Most* of the time scores a 6 in this area. *Sometimes* gets it only a 3, and *hardly ever* doesn't earn a single point.

If your pet can learn new commands in *less* than ten repetitions, it earns 10 points. Twelve repetitions, 8 points; fifteen repetitions, 6 points; twenty repetitions, 2 points.

If your pet has a long-term memory that is able to retain all previous commands without reinforcement, score 10 points. If it occasionally requires reinforcement, drop the score to 8. If it often needs a nudge to remember previous commands, score 3.

If your pet has the ability to solve simple problems, such as going around barriers or finding where you have hidden a favorite toy, it has earned 10 points. If you have to give it a few hints, lower the points earned to 7. If your pet wanders around dazed and confused, sorry, no points on this one.

If your pet demonstrates the ability to adapt quickly to new environments and new situations, you have a smart cookie and it has earned 10 points. If your pet requires a fairly reasonable period of adjustment, give it 7 points. If it wanders around dazed and confused and hasn't a clue, take it home and feed it—but it has earned no points.

- **Scoring:**

80 Points: You have a genius pet that may soon have its own television show. *79–76:* Your pet may pass you in school if you let your homework slide. *75–60:* Your pet needs a little homework and some help from you. *59–49:* You had better spend more time with your pet. *48–38:* Your pet needs lots of love and attention. *37–27:* Your pet needs a dunce cap. *Below 27:* Maybe you brought home a stuffed animal by mistake.

You can increase your pet's intelligence by. . . .

- providing it with new and varied experiences
- keeping its mind active with new commands
- presenting it with new environments
- talking to it during your normal daily routine
- playing various games that encourage interaction without rough-housing
- being consistent in your commands
- showing patience
- giving it lots and lots of love

Select Bibliography:

Balaban, M. and Hill, J. (ed.) *Animal Behavior*. New York: McGraw-Hill, 1969.

Blackemore, C. and Greenfield, S. (ed.) *Mindwaves: Thoughts on Intelligence, Identity and Consciousness*. London: Oxford University Press, 1987.

Bustad, L. *Animals, Aging, and the Aged*. Minneapolis: University of Minnesota Press, 1980.

Caras, R.A. *A Dog Is Listening*. New York: Simon and Schuster, 1993.

Conner, Richard, Ph.D. with Peterson, Dawn. *The Lives of Whales and Dolphins*. New York: Seaver Books, 1994.

Coren, Stanley. *The Intelligence of Dogs, Canine Consciousness and Capabilities*. New York: The Free Press, A Division of MacMillan, Inc., 1994.

Daglish, Eric. *The Life Story of Beasts*. New York: William Morrow and Co., 1931.

Dethier, V.G. and Stellar, E. *Animal Behavior*. Englewood Cliffs, N.J.: Prentice-Hall, 1961.

Dewsbury, Donald, A. *Comparative Animal Behavior*. New York: McGraw-Hill, Inc., 1978.

Dossey, Dr. Larry. *Recovering the Soul—A Scientific and Spiritual Search*. New York: Bantam, 1989.

Evans, Bergen. *The Natural History of Nonsense*. New York: Alfred A. Knopf, Inc., 1946.

Ewer, R.F. *The Carnivores*. Ithaca: Cornell University Press, 1985.

Fiennes, R. and Fiennes, A. *The Natural History of Dogs*. London: Weidenfeld and Nicolson, 1968.

Fogle, B. *The Dog's Mind*. London: Pelham Books, 1990.

Fox, M.W. *Understanding Your Dog*. New York: Coward-McCann, 1982.

Fox, M.W. *Behavior of Wolves, Dogs and Related Canids*. London: Cape, 1985.

Gardner, H. *Theory of Multiple Intelligences*. New York: Basic, 1983.

Green, P. Dale. *Lore of the Dog*. Boston: Houghton Mifflin, 1967.

Griffin, Donald. *Animal Minds*. Chicago: University of Chicago Press, 1992.

Hall, K. and Devore, I. *Primate Behavior: Field Studies of Monkeys and Apes*. New York: Henry Holt & Co., 1965.

Harris, Marvin. *Our Kind*. HarperCollins, 1989.

Hart, B. and Hart, L. *The Perfect Puppy*. New York: W.H. Freeman, 1988.

Krebs, J.R. and Dawkins, R. *Behavioral Ecology: An evolutionary approach*. Sunderland, MA: Sinauer, 1984.

Leach, M. *God Had A Dog*. New Brunswick, N.J.: Rutgers University Press, 1961.

Loeser, Johann. *Animal Behavior*. New York: McGraw-Hill, 1978.

Lorenz, K. *Studies in Animal and Human Behavior*. Cambridge, Harvard University Press, 1971.

Milani, M.M. *The Body Language and Emotion of Dogs*. New York: William Morrow & Co., 1986.

Peterson, Dale and Goodall, Jane. *Visions of Caliban*. New York: Houghton Mifflin, 1993.

Pfaffenberger, C.J. *The New Knowledge of Dog Behavior*. New York: Howell, 1963.

Pribram, Karl. *Languages of the Brain*. New York: Random House, 1982.

Radner, D. and Radner, M. *Animal Consciousness*. Buffalo, N.Y.: Prometheus, 1989.

Rheingold, H.L. *Maternal Behavior in Mammals*. New York: John Wiley and Sons, 1963.

Robbins, John. *Diet for a New America*. Walpole, N.H.: Stillpoint, 1987.

Seton, Ernest Thompson. *Wild Animals I Have Known*. New York: Viking Penguin, 1987.

Sparks, Dr. John. *Parrots: A Natural History*. Facts on File, 1990.

Stemberg, R.J. *The Triarchic Mind: A New Theory of Human Intelligence*. New York: Viking, 1988.

Tortora, D.F. *The Right Dog for You*. New York: Simon and Schuster, 1980.

Watson, Lyall. *Lifetide*. New York: Bantam Books, 1980.

Wilson, E.O. *The Diversity of Life*. Cambridge: Harvard University Press, 1988.

Wilson, E.O. *Sociobiology—The New Synthesis*. Cambridge: Harvard University Press, 1975.

Willoya, William and Brown, Vinson. *Warriors of the Rainbow*. Healdsburg: Naturegraph, 1966.

Zeuner, F.E *History of Domesticated Animals*. New York: Harper & Row 1963.